The Urgency of Holiness in th

Whatever Became of Holiness?

STEVE DENEFF

Edited by:
>   Keith Drury
>   Dave Higle
>   Kelly Trennepohl
>   Gail Whitmire

TABLE OF CONTENTS

ACKNOWLEDGMENT

Plagiarism is the unpardonable literary sin of "stealing from another, certain thoughts, ideas or expressions, and using them as one's own" (Webster).

Guilty! Well, kinda.

In the sense that no man is an island, I am not the sole author of this book. I am only its writer. Directly behind every page are the thoughts, ideas or expressions of other people you have not met.

My father, who taught me first to think, and then to think otherwise, has faithfully advised, defended and prayed for me in the writing of this, and so it bears a certain semblance to his own passion and thought. He is both a hero and a fan to me.

I am indebted to Bret McAtee, my good friend from the reformed tradition, who has batted this subject around with me for hours. His love for truth and his quest for real holiness are refreshing.

. . . and to my staff, Stella Knak and Thad Spring, who ran our church for three months while I ground out the last eight chapters.

. . . and to Keith Drury, whose "keep on keeping on" notes literally pulled the last few chapters out of my tired mind; and to his capable staff, whose penchant for details has saved me a truckload of embarrassment.

. . . and to the congregation at the North Lakeport Wesleyan Church, who endured the many loose ends, missed phone calls, interrupted conversations, and sometimes bad sermons of a busy and distracted pastor who was writing on one subject while preaching on another. They deserve better.

. . . and to my children, Nicholas and Ashley, who allowed me to be on loan to whomever needed me at the time.

. . . and finally, to my beautiful wife, Lori, who faithfully picked up the pieces week after week, so I "wouldn't have to be bothered with them"; who brought umpteen dinners to me at the office; who heard, then polished every tedious thought before it became a chapter; who kept a good and secure home under our feet; and whose servanthood and love for anonymity is such that she will wring my neck for ever having included her in the "acknowledgments."

Sola Dei Gloria!

CHAPTER 1

VIRTUAL HOLINESS

The Tempting of Holiness in the Present Day

In the world of cyberspace, reality has just taken a turn for the worse.

Cyberspace is that ethereal, make-believe world just behind the screen of your computer, or directly under the pad of your keyboard. In 1984, Willie Gibson noticed that computer mavens "accepted almost as an article of faith, that there is some kind of actual space behind the [computer] screen . . . with great warehouses and skyscrapers of data."[1] Gibson called this "cyberspace," and the word stuck.

Today, "cyberspace" is used to describe the invisible network of computers and video imagery which links up the world. It is an invisible room you enter through your computer, where you can do anything from study philosophy, to consult your physician, or book your own hotel reservations. It's a wired, wired world.

And why do we point this out? Because the world of cyberspace offers us a very convincing substitute to real relationships and experiences. It is all style and no substance. It isn't about what's happening. It's what we *think* is happening. But it's all very artificial, and in the end, it leaves our deeper needs unaddressed, all the while claiming to meet them.

There is something of a modern parable here for the church, which finds itself on the brink of a spiritual awakening. In our great quest for truth, we must be sure to grasp what God has for us—and *all* He has for us. It is "true righteousness and holiness" (Ephesians 4:24) we are after, not their pygmy substitutes.

Cyber-Love

In cyberspace, we can talk with anyone we like—our lawyer, priest, senator, doctor or salesman—right over the computer. We can swap recipes, fill prescriptions, earn diplomas, even vote.

Bureaucrats in Washington are eager to go online and swap perspectives with their constituents. Capitol Hill in Washington, D.C., is preparing a "virtual Washington," in which congressmen debate and vote from their own districts. In 1995, Lamar Alexander announced his candidacy for president, over America Online, from his boyhood home in Tennessee. *Newsweek* magazine called it "cyber-announcing . . . no bunting, no pretzels, no beer. Just meet-and-greet with any soul who happens in."

In Bonn, Germany, an electrical engineer has devised a confessional program he calls "Online with Jesus." Back in the USA, we've already had our first online healing service. Supplicants typed in their requests, and a group of pastors and elders tapped out their prayers over the e-mail.

Friends, who have met only on the Internet, will divulge private details about their past. "I told him things I have never told anyone in my life," said one user. "I was really able to be more open. He was able to be more open too." Some time later, the couple met for the first time.[2]

You got it. Bare your soul first. Meet later.

Seems like the cart before the horse, doesn't it?

This is the downside of cyberspace. It poses a threat to our traditional view of love and relationships.

"In cyberspace, you are what you care about [or what you access]," one journalist put it recently. "People will know each other more intimately than ever—and yet not at all." And then he added that despite all the hype, "cyberspace still has a rather empty feel."[3]

Now, the trouble with all of this is that it minimizes friendship to the sharing of information and ideas only. Gone are those interludes where only the silence between us is talking. Gone are the spontaneity and the knowing glances. "Cyber-love," as we will call it, assumes that

8

friendship and affinity for each other is nothing more than the impulse of thought and logic which can be as easily typed as said. It believes that we do not need to watch a person live, so long as we can watch him think. Like I said, reality has taken a turn for the worse.

All of this seems hauntingly similar to the recent craze over morality in the United States. Conservative bureaucrats and pro-this-or-that activists are transmitting their agendas into millions of minds at the speed of light. But there is a certain hollowness to it all, because, even after we have emptied our brains into someone else's, we cannot really say we know that person. The same woman who said she "told him things [she had] never told anyone in [her] life," later met her cyber-lover and found him to be "a very selfish person [who] didn't want to give up anything, but wanted [her] to give up everything."

Fancy that! So, love is an affinity beyond consenting to another person's agenda. We can share the same values and dreams for our community, and even eat from the same tables of literature and philosophy, and *still* not satisfy our need for love. And if all of this seems annoyingly obvious to you, consider that this is precisely what the modern church no longer believes as it stands outside the chambers of power, about ready to sell its birthright of true holiness in exchange for a little moral reform.

Most of the evangelical church today is against abortion. Most of us want pornography outlawed and prayer returned to the classroom. We want Creation taught as a viable science. We want old-fashioned values in our homes, and condoms out of our schools. We want a president or prime minister who prays . . . to *our* God. And no more liberal appointments to the Supreme Court, please. And God help (if we let Him) the tyrant who tries to take away these inalienable rights!

But as we explore this forest of grand ideals, we get the same empty feeling one has when searching for love in cyberspace. These pillars of truth, for which we have been fighting these past hundred years, are a loosely connected and often random set of reactions to an agenda that has been set by others who "do not know the Scriptures or the power of God" (Matthew 22:29).

These things are surely worth an argument. Some are worth fighting for, but none are worth dying for (which many seem ready to do), if we are not first governed by an inward holiness which tests our motives and loves our enemies more than it hates the injustice.

The supreme danger of our day is that the people of God might grab on to one (or more) of these moral hot potatoes and spend all of their energies pushing it forward, somehow believing that this is the hope of the gospel. It might not occur to them that no man can sanctify himself by moralizing his community, and that he who dies in a time of peace, still dies, and will, thereafter, face the holiness of God, at which time his soul will be on the line and his positions on this or that will mean nothing.

Morality Versus Religion

We are not the first generation tempted to moralize our culture, either. During the Second World War, there was talk in Europe of a moral reform, and almost immediately it came under the scrutiny of the church.

Even as piety was swelling in England, C. S. Lewis warned his fellow Christians that, unless they were careful, they might "quietly and gradually [reach] a stage at which religion becomes merely a part of the 'Cause,' in which Christianity is valued chiefly because of the excellent arguments it can produce. . . ." Lewis said if "meetings, pamphlets, policies, movements, causes and crusades [mattered] more to [them] than prayers and sacraments and charity," they had the Devil's religion.[4]

About that same time (1941), D. Martyn Lloyd-Jones delivered a series of lectures to the students of Edinburgh, in which he noted the order and relationship between morality and religion. He concluded, "The order has been reversed: morality has taken precedence over religion . . . but to trust morality alone without religion, or to place morality before religion, leads only to eventual disaster."

With typical precision, Lloyd-Jones proceeded to take the problem apart and state at least six reasons why morality alone is not a sufficient religion.

1. It is an insult to God, for to place anything before God is to deny Him, however noble that thing may be. The blessing of salvation, the moral life, and the improved state of society are the normal consequences of our true belief in God, but they must never be confused with God, himself, who must be worshiped for His own sake, because He is God.

2. It is more interested in a man's actions than in the man, himself. By emphasizing only conduct and behavior, it sacrifices our character and personality on the altar of high standards.

3. It is more interested in society than in the individual, and seeks only to get the individual to conform to the good of the whole. Morality reduces us to a small speck in the huge mass of a nameless and faceless humanity. Religion believes in improving the individuals who compose it. Morality believes in improving the indivual by improving the general state.

4. It insults man by ignoring that which is highest in him: his

relationship to God. Morality deals with us on a lower plane. It may make us a noble and thinking animal, but it knows nothing of men becoming the sons of God.

5. It provides no ultimate authority, but minimizes sin to ignorance, salvation to peace with oneself, and holiness to educating ourselves with Christian virtue. But since these very virtues are themselves based on the thoughts and concensus of man, they are subject to change with each generation.

6. It provides no power to live the good life, and when we have fallen into sin, it merely condemns us, then waits coldly for us to dig ourselves out.[5]

Before we march too deeply into all of this talk about social reform, lives of integrity, conservative agendas and old-fashioned values, we'd better examine again the distinctions between religion and morality, made by men of an earlier day. We ought to consider all the time and energy it will take to run a campaign or carry a flag, and decide whether or not it will lead to lasting holiness or a brief social reform.

For morality only gives us the mistaken notion that we are good people because we hold righteous views. It can convince us that we love God (which is real holiness) merely because we hate evil (which is only moral reform). Morality is a kind of cyber-love for God, in which we measure God's holiness and ours by what each of us cares about. And this makes it seem like we know each other more intimately than ever— even when we do not know each other at all.

The message of holiness for this prodigal generation is not reform, but something more radical. It is that a man's conscience can be as undefiled as his reputation, and his heart as pure as his passion is strong. This, and nothing other or nothing less, is sanctification.

Now there is one other substitute for true holiness that we must avoid.

Using computer imagery, we can shoot the rapids or enter the musty dungeons of the netherworld. We can maneuver an F-16 through enemy fire or perform open-heart surgery on a "virtual cadaver." And all by donning a pair of spectacles that cast a three-dimensional image in front of our eyes.

But virtual reality is no video game. It's real . . . well, almost. Participants go through the motions and emotions of a real experience. They weave about, flail their arms, sweat profusely, and leave the game visibly shaken. But, after an hour or two in the "real world"(?), their heart rate slows, they gradually descend the emotional peak, and soon they are distracted with other things. Nobody hurt. It was all just a game. What a relief!

But they'll be back, because to play the game or to enter the virtual

11

reality often enough is to believe you are there—even when you aren't. It is not just an escape; it becomes an identity with a pseudo-confidence that is developed from having conquered in the other world. All at no risk and little cost. It is a short-term thrill, an affair of style and emotion that gets the adrenaline running and adds excitement to the dull monotony of life.

And did I mention that much of what we call holiness today is but a virtual reality when compared to that more lasting substance of which the Bible speaks? Some will be quite offended to hear me give this imitation "holiness" a name, but much of revivalism, as we know it today, is but a virtual reality, compared to the deeper stuff of perfect love, a well-ordered life and a heart on fire for God.

There are refreshing exceptions, of course. As I write this, a few evangelical colleges are claiming "special times of spiritual awakening," in which "confessions of pride, hatred, lust, sexual immorality, cheating, dishonesty, materialism . . . [are] heard throughout the night [in chapel services]."[6]

But, for the most part, revival has taken a gradual turn from the substantial to the experiential,[7] and the temptation for revivalist churches (as most holiness churches are) is to believe that holiness is just one revival after another. Like I said, this is a holiness of no risk and little cost . . . an affair of style and emotion that gets the adrenaline running and adds excitement to the dull monotony of life. Those who practice this do not always see that true holiness is a long and enduring love for God, in season and out.

Beginning with the Second Great Awakening (1800–1830) and the first frontier camp meetings (at the turn of the nineteenth century), the spiritual fervor of evangelical churches began to be measured increasingly in terms of the churches' emotional impact on their audiences. The most astonishing phenomena at that time were the shouting and barking and laughing and seizures and "treeing the Devil," which usually alerted the audience that something good was about to happen.

No longer were conversion and a return to the Bible the most-talked-about components of the Awakening, as they had been in Jonathan Edwards's, George Whitefield's and John Wesley's day. Read the sermons of John Wesley or Charles Finney, and you will notice their commitment to keeping a tight rein on "enthusiasm."

"Many excitements which are taken for revivals of religion, after all result in very little substantial piety," Finney wrote midway through the 1800s. "Appeals are made too much to the feelings. . . . A strain of preaching is adopted which appeals rather to the sympathies . . . than to the intelligence. A tornado of excitement results, but no intelligent action of the heart."[8]

Within twenty years, the emphasis shifted again to that of faith and physical healing. By the turn of the twentieth century, revival came to mean a sudden outbreak of spiritual fervor, precipitated or followed by signs and wonders.[9]

Each expression was a powerful movement of the Spirit. Each had the counterfeit mixed with the genuine. Each seized the social conscience of America, at least for a time. But each produced a form of virtual holiness, which placed an emphasis on a visible and emotional experience that sometimes obscured the need for a purified heart. In this sense, revivalism has been more smoke than fire.

Nevertheless, as holiness people, we have loved revival and have prayed for it in every generation. But even if our prayers are answered, it will not be enough for today.

A Parable: Days of Power

In the 1860s, the spirituality of America was waning, and cries went up for revival. The "Pastoral Address" of the 1864 Methodist Conference, for example, called publicly for churches to make revival a priority.

According to one observer, those were days when "the ministry conformed to the spirit of the age," on the assumption that "the ministry of the everlasting gospel is to be different in one age from another, [and must] proclaim a gospel modified to suit the ever-varying tastes of humanity." The one trademark of the weakened church was "doctrinal indefiniteness in the pulpit," from which one never heard sermons on law, sin, hell, and, least of all, entire sanctification.

What did they preach about? "Science, philosophy, polite literature, poetry, and even antique fables, constitute much of the material," said the observer. "If we go into the studies of ministers . . . what do we discover? Do we find Wesley and Fletcher and Benson . . . and McCheyne, as their bosom companions? This is not likely. The more popular modern authors, and the lighter literature of the day, are the daily study."

Those ministers who *did* have something to say were often afraid to say it, and so avoided any unpopularity.

Camp meetings fell into "general disrepute." Those who still attended them noticed that "they had become . . . places of recreation and pleasant social intercourse. Families secured their tenting-ground, put up swings for their children, arranged for the favorite croquet game and, in short, prepared for a week or ten days of relaxation in the grove."

Ministers were "seen in the tent door . . . smoking and enjoying jocose (i.e., frivolous, trite) conversation; and this while a handful of devoted men and women were trying to conduct a prayer meeting."

Meanwhile, back in the home church, board members were accepting "worldly policy in the management of church finances." Most collections came in the form of fairs and festivals. And, speaking of money, there was ever the need for more, as the people of God indulged themselves in "church-building mania," the result of which was a "new order of service, corresponding with the building," which was devoid of order and tradition.

Now, it was the conviction of righteous men of the day that this was a defining moment, or, as they called it, a "transition period . . . [in which] two forces diametrically opposed to each other were in dire antagonism." These two forces, they said, were formalism and power. And, in the words of these men, "the cry of the period was undoubtedly for *spiritual power*" (italics in original).[10]

Ten years later, they got exactly what they had asked for (and nothing more) when revival broke out in Vineland, New Jersey. While five hundred were converted and another two hundred sanctified, the real power of the conference was measured in terms of enthusiasm, which is why one official wrote later, "It made every other service seem tame by comparison."[11]

Five years later, the same fellow (J. S. Inskip) changed his mind when he opened the conference that year by praying, "My God, if this is the last camp meeting we shall attend, let it be the best," and then began his sermon an hour later by saying that the last meeting was great, but this one "must be greater."[12] And the danger in all of this (as with any conference or camp meeting today) is that it set a precedent, an expectation, a level of enthusiasm that was, quite frankly, impossible for the local church to perpetuate.

Gradually, such great, enthusiastic meetings became the meaning of revival, until members of the local church began to speak of these meetings as "going to a revival," or as "having revival" themselves. Even now, when one hears of a church on the "brink of revival," one imagines a congregation with high enthusiasm, awaiting the signs and wonders of old.

That Was Then . . . This Is Now!

I have gone into such great detail about that era in history because it so closely rivals our own. And we are confronted with a similar temptation to settle for revival, when what we need is an authentic holiness awakening.

Some of *our* churches have "conformed to the spirit of the age." Some pattern their style of worship after their members' favorite radio station. Others use talk-show sermons or stand-up comedy to invoke the interest of the people. One pastor has recommended getting sermon ideas from the cover of current periodicals because "they tend to be on the cutting edge of the felt needs and fears that people are facing."[13]

Some of *our* pulpits preach a "doctrinal indefiniteness." According to the research of two periodicals, *Pulpit Digest* and *Preaching*, only 24.5 percent of the preachers in evangelical churches today build the "content and organization" of their sermons around "the biblical passage under consideration."[14]

Our preachers preach "science, philosophy, polite literature, poetry, and even antique fables." Devotionals are the most influential books among many ministers today. Other ministers consume from a church management menu. One pastor has had the brilliant idea of "preaching through the *Book of Virtues*" (his words), which is a recent blockbuster book, as I write this, by virtue-crat William Bennett.

As for the accusation of reading works by "the more popular modern authors," I just scanned a list of the most influential books read among forty ministers today, and noted that not one of those books was more than a hundred years old. The Christian church has been publishing now for two thousand years! It is strikingly peculiar when any generation confines its reading to its own century, as ours has done. It is the equivalent of marrying within one's family, and usually has similar consequences.

Some of *our* ministers frolic more than they pray. Twenty-five percent of the ministers in one survey confessed to "inappropriate sexual behavior" with other members of their congregations.

Our boards practice "worldly policy in the management of church finances." If you doubt that, call ten pastors at random and have them read their last month's board meeting agenda to you over the phone. I did. The tally was twenty-eight business items to one spiritual.

Our generation is at the crossroads, too. But our choice is not between formalism and power. It is between mediocrity and holiness.

And we will make a serious mistake if we, like those before us, believe revival will save us. It won't.

It can't.

Here's why.

For starters, revival these days is fairly limited in both its scope and duration, a point Richard Riss makes in his *Survey of 20th-Century Revival Movements*. Writes Riss, "If a society assumes that miracles cannot take place, [then] those within it who experience revivals will probably be restricted either to those who dissent from the prevailing world view or to those who are willing to change their minds about such matters." The rest, who hold anti-supernatural views, "will not take seriously any reports of miraculous outpourings of the Holy Spirit," because they will consider these outpourings to be "outmoded categories of thought."[15]

This is one peculiar difference between our culture and all previous ones. Those of us who are still waiting for the easy answer of revival to unravel all the complex dilemmas of our modern, scientific age ought to consider it, even as we pray.

And even if revival does save our cities, it will be far short of what God intended if it does not purify our souls. Christ does not desire only to put a power surge into our faith, or enthusiasm into our worship. He is not that interested in helping us preach to overflow crowds. His target . . . His purpose . . . His obsession is to purify our hearts, because holiness is a pure heart on fire for God, whether or not anyone shows up to watch it burn.

I do not want to be misunderstood. A revival cannot save us because a revival itself has never saved anyone. The only thing that has (and can) is the message of revival, which is the very gospel of holiness.

Our bout with liberal theology and modernity has left us spiritually bankrupt. Like Samson, we are just now awaking to see that the Lord left us while we were asleep. What is needed is not more power in the church, but more purity. Like Simon the Sorcerer, we and our money will perish if we think we can buy the gift of God with revival alone. So, in between our prayers for revival, let us mark it down that there will be no baptism of the Spirit until those who would be baptized will first disrobe their old and sinful natures, and lay them down in total surrender. This we call sanctification. And it is really more than semantics.

The only hope for our churches, our theology, our colleges, and especially our own souls, is a renewed vision of the holiness of God. Then, we need a clear picture of our own sinful pride, lust, complacency, or elitism that is not a virtual reality, but a *real* one. We need a religion we cannot play at. We need an obsession with grace that pushes itself into every inch of our overcrowded lives, and throws the competition out. We need to treat the Holy as holy again. Like Luther, we need to tremble again as we open the Scriptures or break the bread.

This holy fear of God will save anybody, and it will save us. But don't mistake it for something like spiritual power or a second blessing. This is not a cry for revival, with man at the center, but for a vision of God and holiness, with Christ at the center.

What? Another Book on Holiness?

This book begins there. It assumes that, unlike previous generations, we cannot jump suddenly into a conversation about a second blessing with a culture that misunderstands the first. *Justification, sanctification,* and *holiness* all mean different things, but each has its roots in the holiness of God. Therefore, we must begin there and work forward through our understanding of sin, repentance, salvation, sanctification, and a life of holiness.

This is not a book on theology, though there is some of that here. This is a book about practical holiness and experiential grace, written both to afflict the comfortable and to comfort the afflicted. I hope you can feel a little of the passion and agony that went into every page. I have tried to write it *with* the head, yet *from* the heart. I have bled a little here. I would hope that you bleed some, too. For in spite of how often we struggle and fail and frustrate ourselves, a thorough examination is still worth the effort, and the message of the whole gospel is that somehow a higher life is possible and that we can have it even in this world.

C. S. Lewis once observed that we are too easily pleased. We are "like an ignorant child who wants to go on making mud pies in a slum," he said, "because we cannot imagine what is meant by the offer of a holiday at the sea."

Let us be true to God and to ourselves. Let us not squander this important hour on lesser things, but let us carefully examine the testimony we are handing our children. If we don't, we will not only ruin our day, but theirs. For the sun will rise tomorrow like it sets tonight.

If this is not enough, let us remember that we are in a battle for our own souls here, and when we decide the fate of holiness for this generation, we are, in that moment, deciding everything else.

And afterward, we will have all of eternity to ponder our decision.

NOTES:
[1] Philip Elmer-DeWitt, "Welcome to Cyberspace," *Time* Special Edition (March 1995): p. 4.
[2] Jill Smolowe, "Intimate Strangers," *Time* Special Edition (March 1995): pp. 21, 24.
[3] Howard Fineman, "The Brave World of Cybertribes," *Newsweek* (February 27, 1995): p. 30.
[4] C. S. Lewis's short essays first appeared in *The Guardian,* a now-extinct periodical in England during the Second World War, and were reprinted later with only minor revisions in *The Screwtape Letters* (New York: MacMillan, 1961), p. 35.

[5] D. Martyn Lloyd-Jones, *The Plight of Man and the Power of God* (Grand Rapids: Baker, 1982), pp. 25–40.

[6] Taken from a memo by Chaplain Kellough to the faculty and staff of Wheaton College. Cited in "Divine Initiative," *World Magazine* (April 15, 1995): p. 25.

[7] See Richard M. Riss's *Survey of 20th-Century Revival Movements* (Peabody: Hendrickson, 1988), pp. 1–30. In the first two chapters, Riss offers a good summary of the shift from doctrine to experience in modern revivalism.

[8] Shortly after the Second Awakening (1800–1830), Charles Finney composed a series of "open letters" on the criticism and excesses of revivals. These letters were first published in the *Oberlin Evangelist* in 1845–46, and later as a book, even before the evangelist's death. Unfortunately, most of Finney's readers today are more familiar with his *Lectures on Revival* and *Systematic Theology* than his later, and more mature, series of reflections called *Letters on Revival*. Copies of these letters still may be found, under various titles. My copy is titled *Reflections on Revival, by Donald Dayton, comp.* (Minneapolis: Bethany Fellowship, 1979), p. 43, from which this statement is taken.

[9] In Donald Dayton's *Theological Roots of Pentecostalism* (Peabody: Hendrickson, 1987), pp. 15–34, the author discusses the progression of revival through the four major themes of early holiness theology: **(1) Instantaneous Salvation** (which was the emphasis of crisis-theology in the Second Awakening [1800–1830]); **(2) Baptism of the Spirit** (which was the emphasis of Holiness Revivals [1840–1870]); **(3) Healings and Miracles** (which was the emphasis of Higher-Life or Post-Civil War Revivalism under such leaders as J. I. Inskip, Oscar Cullis, A. J. Gordon, A. B. Simpson and others [1870–1895]); and, finally, **(4) the Second Coming of Christ, or Premillennialism** (which was the emphasis of the Neo-(or New) Pentecostal Revivals [1914], and the Latter-Rain Revivals [1940s]). In surveying the history of revivalism inside the holiness tradition, one notices that while every revival has included each of these four themes, we have somewhat shifted the emphasis from one to the next over the years, and often at the expense of the previous doctrine.

[10] These observations were recorded by George Hughes in *Days of Power in the Forest Temple* (Boston: John Bent & Co., 1873), pp. 3–40. According to Hughes, these were the social conditions which precipitated the post-Civil War revival, and the subsequent rise of the National Camp Meetings for the Promotion of Holiness.

[11] Cited by Richard Riss in *A Survey of 20th Century Revival Movements*. See also Melvin Dieter's chapter, "The Post-Civil War Holiness Revival," in *Reformers and Revivalists* (Indianapolis: Wesley Press, 1992), pp. 150–182.

[12] Taken from the minutes of the 1870 Holiness Camp Meeting in Landisville, PA. Recorded by Adam Wallace in *A Modern Pentecost* (Salem: H. E. Schmul, 1970), pp. 22, 25.

[13] Taken from *The Baby Boomerang*, by Doug Murren. Cited by John MacArthur in *Ashamed of the Gospel* (Wheaton: Crossway, 1993), p. 120.

[14] Cited by David Wells in *No Place for Truth* (Grand Rapids: Eerdmans, 1993), p. 251.

[15] Richard Riss, *A Survey of 20th-Century Revival Movements*, pp. 2–3.

CHAPTER 2

FOR HE'S A JOLLY GOOD FELLOW

The Humanization of God and the Rediscovery of His Holiness

I once asked a young man if he'd ever thought about dying and what he expected to be doing when that time came. He smiled confidently as he leaned back in his chair, folded his arms and said, "Just lying there like this with a smile on my face, thinking about God."

Unbelievable!

Holy men of the Bible may have trembled at the thought of meeting God, and Augustine may have died reciting the Confessions, but this young man plans to barge into eternity with no thought of what may be required of him after he is dead.

Survey after survey reveals the same paradox. Nearly everyone believes in God. Nearly everyone believes he is going to heaven. Yet three-fourths of them (or more) fail in the questions which test their ethics. One study found that seventy percent of the people surveyed believed that it is "very important to do what God and the Scriptures say when choosing between right and wrong," yet two-thirds of this group rejected the idea of moral absolutes. Figure that out!

The best explanation is that we have created a subjective God out of the ashes of the past forty years who, like Jeremiah's "scarecrow in a melon patch" (Jeremiah 10:5), can be moved safely into certain areas of our lives and out of others. This God is the god of good feelings and high ideals. He is politically correct. The new God loves the homosexual, but hates the moralist. He'll tolerate abortion, but never child abuse. He is honored to have us take His Sacraments in the sanctuary, but hardly notices moments later when we take His name in vain in the parking lot.

Our modern Deity is kinder, gentler, and more tolerant than the heavenly tyrant of the last century. He is the perfect countryman. He espouses every view and no view, all at once. He is all grace, so no grace is necessary. He is love without discrimination, mercy without law, power without intimidation, knowledge without conviction, truth without an attitude. He might even be a "she."

Like a mother whose children have outgrown her and moved away, He waits for us to call Him every Sunday and flatter Him with sermons and doxologies. He is proud of His children, but He no longer controls them. They are big now and have minds of their own. And as such, they are free to define Him in any way they please. For instance,

- three out of every ten adults, some of whom identify themselves as "Christian," believe God is only "the realization of all human potential . . . a state of higher consciousness that a person can reach."[1]
- "God is not perfect" say a growing number of Americans, according to George Barna. While most still believe Jesus was the son of God, forty-two percent of them say He committed sins while He was on earth.[2]
- a gay rights conference in Washington gathered under a banner which read "If Jesus were here, he'd march too!"[3]
- a prominent leader of the men's movement scolded the church for insisting that men follow a code of moral conduct, rather than "appropriating the love and forgiveness of the Father-God."[4]

When did the "Holy One of Israel" become the jolly good fellow He is today?

The God of the Bible is very different. He is merciful and slow to anger. But He is also holy and just. He is uncompromising. He is unapproachable light, exposing our sins and condemning whatever sin He does not cleanse. This makes us feel paranoid, like someone is watching us through the keyhole while we carry on with acts we think are done in private. It strikes fear and trembling, neither of which have much place in modern religion. Actually, a vision of God's holiness has many effects, but it never allows me to sit there "with a smile on my face, thinking about God."

Six Side-Effects of God-Shrinking

Just as a clear vision of God's holiness has profound effects on any culture, so a cloudy vision of God's holiness has its implications as well.

One tragedy peculiar to our modern culture is that low views of God have slipped into the mainstream of Christian thought. Even among the rank and file, one hears references to "the man upstairs" or "Big Daddy" or, more commonly, "the good Lord"—which is a proverbial pat on the head. Those who use these terms say that these phrases are only benign colloquialisms. Yet, one wonders if they are more of a Freudian slip.

We have come a long way from earlier days when people trembled and the earth shook at the mention of God's name. Nobody I know shudders at the thought of mispronouncing the name *Yahweh,* and the fact that some from an earlier day did shudder seems like mere superstition to us who claim to be enlightened. The result has been a society in disarray, running here and there to cure the symptoms of a terminal disease we refuse to admit. But consider, for a moment, some of the logical consequences of any culture that forfeits its doctrine of the holiness of God. It is a perfect description of our present condition which, at best, is critical.

First, where there are low views of God, **there is no law,** for law is based on a commonly accepted morality. The United States Constitution calls this an "inalienable right." Lawyers call it "natural law." Today we call it "common-sense morality." It is the assumption that there are certain absolutes which are true for all people, during all times, and in all places. These are nonnegotiable presuppositions which underlie every other law. They are basic principles built into every human being, regardless of age, culture, intelligence or environment. An example would be the "right to life (and) liberty," as stated in the Preamble to the Constitution and in the Bill of Rights.

But such absolutes are always founded on a "standard," which is the idea that there is someone, somewhere who already embodies what the rest of us want to become. In this sense, improvement is measured by whether or not one is moving closer to the standard.

Now, if God is not holy, then He is more like us and less like a standard. He is "in progress," the same as we are. And if God is not the standard, there is none. If there is no standard, we are moving neither closer nor further from the truth, so reason itself is suspect and hostage to the numberless special interest groups who will rush in to fill the void. This is what prompted the agnostic Friederich Nietzche to suggest that in the absence of God, all that is left us is power.

So there can be no laws unless there is Someone fit to make them. Perhaps this is why God first established His own holiness before laying down the laws in Exodus or Leviticus.

A second consequence of the humanization of God is that **there is no sin,** but only "alternative lifestyles" and minor aberrations to goodness. For if God is like us, sin is an opinion, rather than a transgression of the law; and guilt is only a roadblock, rather than the ditches on the road to happiness and freedom. We will discuss this more in the next chapter.

Third, where God is not holy, **there is little incentive to change our behavior.** We merely accept whatever we have become. As we already have argued, there is no reason to change. Our lifestyles and opinions are as good as any others'.

Fourth, if God is not holy, **there is no gospel.** If there is no law, no sin, and no incentive to change, the church has nothing to offer the world. We are not "a chosen people and royal priesthood" if we are not "a holy nation" (1 Peter 2:9), for we will be just like everybody else.

What do we tell the recovering alcoholic or the decrepit old man dying in the shadows of a convalescent home? What hope do we hold for those who have ruined their lives up to now? Are we not only the blind leading the blind? Isn't our opinion only one among many in the marketplace of ideas, if God is not holy? For what, then, makes *His* message any better?

If we would reach the world with a gospel that is still "the power of God for the salvation of everyone who believes" (Romans 1:16) . . . if the world would take us seriously again . . . we must offer them something worthwhile and better than themselves.

Fifth, if we forfeit the doctrine of the holiness of God, **there is a lower level of commitment among those who would be Christians.** This is the sum total of all previous consequences. If God is not holy, there is nothing out there impressive enough to demand our time and attention. If God is not a "consuming fire" (Hebrews 12:29), then He will have to take His place next to the Girl Scouts and the PTA as just another resource to help improve our community; and the church will have to jockey for the interest of a society that is equally devoted to all of these organizations.

From these consequences, it is evident that the Devil does not need to make atheists of us in order to win the day. He only needs to remove the idea of the holiness of God from our platforms, bookshelves, seminaries and consciences, and we will soon after make atheists of ourselves.

There is still one more consequence of minimizing the holiness of God. It is this: **the whole doctrine of God disintegrates** if His holiness is diminished.

The early Puritan writer, Stephen Charnock, pointed out that the holiness of God is the one attribute behind every other. According to Charnock, God's holiness was first on God's mind, for it was the only attribute repeated in threefold succession—"holy, holy, holy is the Lord God Almighty" (Revelation 4:8); it was the only one He swore by— "once for all I have sworn by my holiness" (Psalm 89:35); it was the very essence of God, himself—"be holy because I am holy" (Leviticus 11:44); and is thus the first virtue He desires to re-create in us.

His holiness is what makes Him "God." It is the moral center or nucleus to everything else about Him. If we lose or diminish it, we are left not with another kind of God, but with no God at all.

For instance, if we say God is *love,* but do not tie it to His holiness, then His love lacks discretion, which means it is only foolish sentiment.

To say He is *just,* but not holy, is an oxymoron, since justice implies both a standard and the right to uphold it.

And if we insist God is *merciful,* but ignore His holiness, we have defeated the need for mercy in the first place, since He cannot justly condemn us if He is not perfect himself.

Without holiness, God's *goodness* lacks purpose and direction and is, arguably, not real goodness at all, but only random benevolence. For goodness to be truly "good," it must be consistent with character, or be headed in the direction of a greater goal. But unless God is holy, He has no character, and there is no goal.

To say that God knows and sees everything *(omniscience)* has little significance unless His holiness allows Him to judge everything. And His *omnipotence* (or sovereign power) is tyranny in the absence of holy character, since it is subject to temperament or moods.

So God's holiness is the double-edged sword which brings fear into our fascination of Him. It is the one attribute that makes Him perfect. Complete. Untamed. It is no wonder that those who see it recoil and come to loathe themselves.

Adam and Eve hid from God's holiness in the Garden of Eden. Moses covered his face. The people of Israel kept at a safe distance. The accusations of Job melted into worship under its heat. The Prophet Daniel and the Apostle John stood before it until they could stand no longer; then "fell at his feet as though dead" (Revelation 1:17). And Peter felt its penetrating gaze right after his third denial, then "went outside and wept bitterly" (Luke 22:62).

Whenever a man stares into the holiness of God, it is *man* who blinks first. The one thing he does not do is sit there "with a smile on [his] face, thinking about God."

But God's holiness has a friendly side as well. It motivates us to change—to do better. It says, "follow me" and "do as I do." God is not the little-league father who never played the game, yet expects a highlight film out of his son. God is the perfect example of what He wants us to become. And He wants it, not because He is stuck on himself, but because the holy life is the normal employment of ordinary people who haven't forgotten that they are human, as well as saints.

Rediscovering the Holiness of God

Think of the many attributes of God as spokes on a wheel which, if you follow their reasoning long enough, will take you back to the hub of His holiness. As spokes emanate from the hub, so the attributes of God emanate from His holiness, which brings them all together in an orderly fashion. Yet most of us appreciate the other attributes (love, justice, mercy, goodness) more.

That was the case once in Israel. Who can forget Isaiah's vision of God in the Temple (see Isaiah 6:1-8)? But what many ignore is that this vision occurred during a time of great distress when everyone was focused on Tiglath-Pileser, the mighty Assyrian king who was sweeping south into Israel, gobbling one city after another (2 Kings 15:29). Jerusalem was buzzing. The people trembled. Who would keep the bloodthirsty Assyrians from ransacking the city? Isaiah's own visit to the Temple was, quite possibly, associated with a national cry for God to intervene and save the city from destruction. The prayers of the day were for God's sovereignty, justice and faithfulness.

But in striking contrast to all that was happening in Jerusalem, the scene in heaven (see Isaiah 6) was not one of panic or wrath, but of serenity. In the middle of a crisis, the angels were not throwing lightning to the earth. They were covering their faces and feet, worshiping God— not because nothing else mattered, but because nothing else mattered *more*. All of heaven was obsessed with the holiness of God.

The same was true in the Revelation. God's throne was surrounded by lightning, thunder and fire. But as the Apostle John passed through this hurricane of activity into its eye, he noticed the calm, yet compulsive worship of four living creatures who cried "Holy, holy, holy is the Lord God Almighty" (Revelation 4:8). Even as the earth disintegrated under plagues and wars, their worship continued. They were oblivious to anything else. The meaning is clear: the epicenter of heaven is the holiness of God.

Isaiah's rare interlude of insight had a stunning effect. The consequences of his vision, and the sequence of them, provide a pretty good outline of what to expect when we rediscover the holiness of God.

1. First, where God's holiness is observed, **the Lord is "high and exhalted"** (Isaiah 6:1). He ceases to be the private possession of a few people who live inside a certain denomination or era in history. He is bigger than life. This inspires real and spontaneous worship, as opposed to the happy euphoria produced by music or mood. It maximizes our faith. We remember "nothing is impossible with God" (Luke 1:37). It brings heroics back to our religion. The people of God enlist to help Him win the conflict over evil. All of this happens when the Lord is lifted up.

2. A moment later, **we are humbled.** This is the second effect of God's holiness upon the watching saint. One of the peculiarities of Isaiah's account is that it is dated "in the year that King Uzziah died" (Isaiah 6:1). The irony is that while it was common for prophets to date their calling by the year of a king's reign (Jeremiah, Daniel, Amos, Haggai and Zechariah all did), it was unusual to date it by the *death* of a king. Even more confusing is the fact that Uzziah wasn't even king when he died. Jotham was. So why would Isaiah associate his calling with Uzziah's death instead of Jotham's reign? It was because of the manner in which Uzziah died.

Second Chronicles tells the story of a young, sixteen-year-old boy who became king and succeeded beyond the measure of most before him. He was rich, famous and powerful. That was the problem.

For, once he was king, Uzziah entered the Temple to burn incense on the golden altar (a privilege reserved for priests alone) and was struck with leprosy while he stood there. The Jewish historian, Josephus, tells us that Uzziah was smitten when he threatened to kill the eighty priests, who were already warning him to leave. But, after being stricken with leprosy, he left the Temple and moved outside the city, while his son, Jotham, reigned as king. In less than a year, Uzziah was dead and was "buried by himself in his own gardens" . . . a sad ending to an illustrious career.[5]

As the Prophet Isaiah stood in the Temple where Uzziah was cursed, he must have replayed the mental videos of that tragic day and remembered that the holiness of God is never to be presumed upon. For it was here that God drew a memorable line of distinction between himself and the creature. Isaiah would not have missed the point.

God was "high and exalted"; Uzziah was wasting away outside the city. God was "seated on a throne"; Uzziah had lost his. God's robe filled the Temple; Uzziah's was already in another king's closet. God was "holy, holy, holy"; Uzziah shouted "unclean, unclean" each time he left the compound. God was glorified by a multitude; Uzziah was backing up into his grave.

Each time we meditate on the holiness of God, each time He enters the room where we are worshiping, we are struck first with His greatness, and then with our own unworthiness. These two always go together, and should.

"Genuine worshipers want to blot themselves out of the picture," wrote J. I. Packer, "so that all can concentrate, without distraction, on God alone." And these people have learned they cannot exalt themselves and God at the same time.

3. As this happens, as the glory of God sucks the wind out of our self-inflated sails, **we are smitten with a sense of our sinfulness.** "Woe is me," cried the prophet, "I am ruined." He did *not* say, "I need help." Whenever we gaze into God's purity, we begin to feel not only unworthy, but sinful. In fact, our estimation of God and of sin usually work in opposite proportion. The secret thought or passion which lurks in the dark caverns of our soul, the heart which no man can know, is suddenly exposed to a blinding light. Samuel Logan Brengle wrote,

"I saw the humility of Jesus, and my pride; the meekness of Jesus, and my temper; the lowliness of Jesus, and my ambition; the faithfulness of Jesus, and the deceitfulness of my heart; the unselfishness of Jesus, and my selfishness; the trust and faith of Jesus, and my doubts and unbelief . . . I got my eyes off everybody but Jesus and myself, and I came to loathe myself."[6]

There is a great deal of talk these days about getting the world to see its sin. We preach sermons, run crusades, control worship, sponsor twelve-step groups; some even carry "turn or burn" sandwich boards around the ballpark. But genuine repentance is not the product of mood, fear, or guilt for having broken a faceless law, but of remorse for having offended the Holy One behind it. A spiritual brokenness, a keen sense of our total depravity, cannot be taught or given away; it must be discovered one convert at a time. So, the revival for which the church has prayed for years is less dependent upon anything we can muster, and more on whether or not we rediscover the holiness of God.

I have come to believe the primary objective of any youth or children's ministry is to impart to them the fear and reverence of the Lord . . . a God-consciousness that says we are never alone, but always under His gaze. It may not cure every evil of adolescence, but it is at least something substantial upon which we can build convictions in the coming years.

4. Those who have grasped the holiness of God inherit **grace and**

forgiveness. Actually, these are the last things one would expect to see, yet they are God's first response. But the sequence here is critical. It was *after* the prophet repented that he was forgiven, and not before. It was the very part he surrendered which the angel purified. One would expect a prophet who had just confessed to total "ruin" and "unclean lips" to feel worse than anyone. But the opposite is true. Not only does he acknowledge his cleansing, but he even volunteers for service before the day is over. This is the final link in the miracle of Isaiah's Temple day. We should remember it well: once we are forgiven . . .

5. We are **called into service** . . . by the same vision which first humiliated us. This is the supreme irony. We have a natural aversion to God's holiness, which sends us into hiding. Yet, if we are willing to take a chance and stare down the grim prospects, we are not ruined or ridiculed, but accepted and invited to serve.

Again, the sequence here is also critical. God's holiness *must* humble before it recruits.

But our pattern in the last 40 years has been something else. During the Church Growth Movement of the late sixties, the emphasis of the church shifted from repentance to recruitment. The term *evangelism* gradually came to mean "getting them to come to church." In reality, it meant "getting their attention." Nearly all of us assumed that conversion would follow as we focused on discipling those who were then interested. But it didn't.

Instead of evangelizing those we had, we doubled our efforts to recruit even more. Soon after, we developed an emphasis on the discovery and implementation of spiritual gifts. Most of the material in this area was developed between 1972 and 1978—only three to five years after the rise of the Church Growth Movement in North America.

It is easy to see where this has taken us. We have recruited, mobilized, and elected into power thousands of people who were never truly converted in the first place. Hereafter, the prospects of ever confronting them with the authenticity of their conversion are slim to none. Our recruits are deep in the quagmire of hollow performance.

Read again Isaiah's words (from Isaiah 6:1-8):

In the year that King Uzziah died, I saw the Lord seated on a throne, high and exalted, and the train of his robe filled the temple. Above him were seraphs, each with six wings: With two wings they covered their faces, with two they covered their feet, and with two they were flying. And they were calling to one another: "Holy, holy, holy is the LORD Almighty; the whole earth is full of his glory." At the sound of their voices the doorposts and thresholds shook and the temple was filled with smoke. "Woe to me!" I cried. "I am ruined! For I am a man of unclean lips, and I live among a people of unclean lips, and my eyes have seen the King, the LORD Almighty." Then one of the seraphs flew to me with a live coal in his hand, which he had taken with tongs from the altar. With it he touched my mouth and said, "See, this has touched your lips; your guilt is taken away and your sin atoned for." Then I heard the voice of the Lord saying, "Whom shall I send? And who will go for us?" And I said, "Here am I. Send me!"

First we catch a new vision of God's holiness and our own unworthiness (vv. 1-3), *then* we are smitten with a sense of our own sinfulness (v. 5), *then* God forgives and converts us (vv. 6-7), *and finally*, He drafts us into His service (v. 8). Unless we are renewed in this order, we are better left alone.

More than anything, the new believer, the dying church, the fence-sitter, the political piranha, and the discouraged minister need an unveiled look at the holiness of God. It is not a cure-all. But it is the most accurate and concise prescription we have.

And now comes the hard part.

Has Anyone Seen God Lately?

Once we believe the rediscovery of God's holiness is the solution to nearly every problem of modern faith, we are tempted to rush out and find a formula to discover God's holiness and solve our problems. But the answer is not as easy or clear as we would like.

The truth is, from the stories of those in the Bible and in later centuries who were shown a vision (literal or symbolic) of the holiness of God, no clear formula emerges. There is no list of things to do. No prayers to be said. No orders of worship. No sacred places. No "must-read" books.

There is only a habit. And it might be said that we are quite bad at it. It is the habit of *solitude*.

In every case where God was rediscovered, men were silent and alone. Isaiah spent a day in the Temple. Daniel, three weeks by the river. John, a season on Patmos. Bunyan, years in prison. Finney, a day in the woods. Brengle, a week in his bedroom.

It has been said that no great work in literature or in science was ever wrought by a man who did not love solitude. We may lay it down as an elemental principle of religion, that no large growth in holiness was ever gained by one who did not take time to be often long alone with God.[7]

Next to the fact that Jesus was God, the single most significant source of His power and purity was, as Luke observed, that Jesus "often withdrew to lonely places and prayed" (Luke 5:16). It is no different for us. Try as we will, we simply cannot have the meat of our faith at the drive-through window. It is discipline and hard work, which require much more than just sitting there "with a smile on my face, thinking about God."

In 1961, after A. W. Tozer had "preached himself off of every Bible conference platform in the country,"[8] he was granted the privilege of speaking to a conference of ministers on the subject of his choice. Predictably, the doctrine of God's holiness was not far from his mind. "I believe we ought to have again the old biblical concept of God which makes God awful and makes men lie face down and cry, 'Holy, holy, holy, Lord God Almighty,'" he told his audience that night. "That would do more for the church than everything or anything else."[9]

Within a year, Tozer suffered a heart attack and was ushered into the presence of the very One about whom He spoke. He would see with his eyes what only his heart had known up to that time. And he would know firsthand that whatever else may have been said about his fiery sermon that night, he had not overstated his case.

NOTES:
[1] George Barna, *America Renews Its Search* (Ventura, CA: Regal Books, 1992), p. 75.

[2] *National & International Religion Report* (November 28, 1994): p. 2.

[3] *National & International Religion Report* (May 3, 1993): p. 7.

[4] From an address by Gordon Dalbey to a San Diego Christian Conference on trauma and sexuality. Taken from *National & International Religion Report* (May 16, 1994): p. 4.

[5] Flavius Josephus, *Antiquities of the Jews,* 9:10:4. Taken from the single volume *The Works of Josephus* (Peabody: Hendrickson, 1987), p. 261.

[6] Clarence W. Hall, *Samuel Logan Brengle: Portrait of a Prophet* (New York: Salvation Army, 1933), pp. 47–48.

[7] Cited by Donald Whitney in *Disciplines of the Christian Life* (Colorado Springs: NavPress, 1991), p. 186.

[8] From the introduction by Warren Wiersbe to *A Treasury of A. W. Tozer* (Grand Rapids: Baker, 1980), p. 8.

[9] A. W. Tozer, "Worship: the Missing Jewel in the Evangelical Church," in *The Best of A. W. Tozer,* comp. by Warren Wiersbe (Harrisburg: Christian Publications, 1978), p. 219.

CHAPTER 3

DIRTY ROTTEN SCOUNDRELS

The Trivialization of Sin and the Death of Conscience

The apologist, G. K. Chesterton, once said the doctrine of original sin was the one belief empirically validated by thirty-five hundred years of human history.

But the old doctrine has fallen on hard times lately. Not because we have bettered ourselves, nor even because we have denied it, but because we have given it another name besides "sin," another meaning besides "rebellion," another perpetrator besides "self," another enemy besides God, and another cure besides "atonement."

If you doubt that, read your newspaper.

A man from Boston was acquitted of flying illegal drugs into the United States because he suffered from "action addict syndrome," an emotional imbalance that makes a man crave dangerous adventure.

A mob of young men in Miami robbed, beat, then shot to death a middle-aged man as he stopped for an accident in their neighborhood. Witnesses say the robbery of twenty-seven dollars from the victim's pocket was a secondary motive. The real culprit? "Young men in the neighborhood have too many guns and too much time on their hands," said one reporter.[1]

Riots in Los Angeles have been blamed on "racial tension, poverty and unemployment," yet hundreds from the affluent suburbs have been seen loading the spoils into their Lexus and BMW automobiles to drive away. Less than half of those arrested for these crimes were poor, black or unemployed.

Another man from Oregon who tried to kill his wife was acquitted because he suffered from "depression suicide syndrome." That is, he "deliberately committed a poorly planned crime with the unconscious goal of being caught or killed."[2]

If it is true that the last stage of compromise is to empty words of their traditional meanings and fill them with new meanings, we've got to be living inside the two-minute warning here.

Whatever Became of Sin?

Twenty years ago, Karl Menninger sounded the buzzer with his bestseller, *Whatever Became of Sin?* The title alone is the most often quoted part of the book, but the loaded questions come later.

[Sin] was once a word in everyone's mind, but now rarely if ever heard. Does that mean that no sin is involved in all our troubles—sin with an "I" in the middle? Is no one any longer guilty of anything? Guilty perhaps of a sin that could be repented and repaired and atoned for? Is it only that someone may be stupid or sick or criminal or asleep? . . . Anxiety and depression we all acknowledge, and even vague guilt feelings; but has no one committed any sins? Where, indeed, did sin go? What became of it?[3]

The short answer is that "sin" presupposes first a God and later a confrontation with Him. It implies that God is better than we thought, and we are worse. It means the condemnation of "me, a sinner" for which "God have mercy" is the only way out (Luke 18:13). For most, this is a dreadful thought. But, for the proud heart, there are two ways out. One is to live up to a standard. The other is to lower the expectations. This is precisely the course we have taken recently, through a variety of methods.

A Loss of the Holy

First, and this is the most important here, **we have diminished the holiness of God.** The Bible says we were created in God's image, and not in His place. This means, among other things, that we must measure our own worth against that of God. We know who *we* are because we know who *He* is. This puts the glory of men and the glory of God on opposite ends, pulling against one another.

So, as a rule, the less we think of God, the better we think of ourselves. And if God is the jolly good fellow we think He is, we have less to feel sorry for and nothing to fear. So the doctrines of holiness and sin either rise or fall together. What we do to the one, we have done—whether knowingly or unknowingly—to the other.

It is no surprise, then, that the same culture which began telling us God was dead, later told us sin was only the manifestation of our lower nature, which we must cease to patronize. Then, later still, this same culture thumbed its nose at the world in Nuremberg, by insisting we had no right to force the doctrine of "natural law" (most notably, the sanctity of life) onto another society.

Thus did Germany vindicate itself of the slaughter of six million Jews in the Second World War. The Holocaust may have been fueled by the Aryan conspiracy, but its defense was well founded in the liberal theology of the day, upon which the tormentors feasted. Anyone paying attention to the line of thought in that culture's past seventy-five years should have seen it coming.

Anytime we diminish the holiness of God, we have nothing to shoot for. After all, if God has problems, He certainly cannot condemn us for ours.

Now, if we have nothing to shoot for, we can never really miss. We may commit crimes or make mistakes or suffer addictions or choose the lesser of evils, but we cannot sin—since *sin* is peculiarly a religious term.

If we have not sinned, we need not repent.

If we need not repent, we cannot be forgiven.

If we cannot be forgiven, we cannot be delivered.

And here is the rub: if we cannot be delivered, we can never change. We are forever trapped in a downward spiral of sin, habit, and finally, addiction—with no savior but therapy, the only hope for those without God in this world. This explains the brisk sales of self-help psychology books among secular bookstores. It does not, however, explain it among Christian authors, whose readers are supposed to believe in repentance. But it is all we can expect when our religion loses its sense of the mystical. Our only prayer is like that of the agnostic who said, "Oh God . . . if there is a God; save my soul . . . if I have a soul."

There simply *must* be an absolute standard, a perfect measurement, a straight edge. We cannot just flit from one generation to the next, eyeballing it. If we are to keep our moral sanity, there must be a place where all truth meets; an ultimate purpose behind the ever-changing laws; a highest court, beyond which there is no appeal. For anytime we lessen the holiness of God, we have sold the ground out from under our feet.

The Vanishing Conscience

A second reason for the disappearance of sin is our **elimination of guilt.** Many people who feel guilty, *should*, but are not allowed the luxury because some able psychologist has explained it all away with the fig leaf of modern psychotherapy. The Prophet Jeremiah said, "they do not even know how to blush" (Jeremiah 6:15).

While Jesus often started with psychological problems and worked toward spiritual answers (the woman with five husbands, the woman caught in adultery, and the disciples on the road to Emmaus are three examples), the "modus operandi" of many, even Christian, psychologists is exactly the opposite. They often begin with what is clearly a *spiritual* problem, for which the Bible offers clear counsel, then drag it onto their home field by diagnosing it with their own terminology, never looking for the deeper problems of pride, rebellion or unbelief.

The Bible itself is often hostage to the presuppositions of psychologists, most of whom have not taken a single course in theology or hermeneutics. When I reminded one woman that "the truth would set her free," she retorted with an almost gnostic confidence that her emotional scars of the past were somehow blocking the truth from getting past her head and into her heart. The Bible calls her condition "unbelief." But, once we surrendered the terminology to the clinicians, we lost the right to treat the problem.

Secular sociologist Vicki Abt has satirized . . . [The] "therapeutic view of evil as sickness, not sin, is the basis of co-dependency theory. . . . Recovery is a process that holds the promise of secular redemption. No matter how many days you've consumed, how irresponsibly you've behaved, how much corruption enjoyed, you can be reborn and get in touch with the innocent child inside that has remained untouched by the worst of your sins. . . . There is a relentless optimism that is devoid of negative messages of guilt or shame."[4]

All of this leaves many "seekers" well-adjusted, but still dead in their sins; and it leaves the church, as analyst M. Scott Horton put it, as "mere interns to the real doctors of the American soul." Unless we continue to preach and believe in personal sin, we will only anesthetize our guilt, rather than heed it as the warning it is, and so deprive ourselves of our most compelling reason to repent and find forgiveness.

Defining Deviancy Down

A third reason we are sin-less these days is our capacity to, as one writer put it, **"define deviancy down."**[5] As a culture becomes submerged in evil, goes the theory, it reaches a point where the prognosis is so dismal, the chances for recovery so grim, the "way back" so long and overwhelming, that it unconsciously surrenders the norm by dividing its evils into two categories: sins and errors. As each category becomes more cluttered (or common), we add a third category labeled "normal." Now there are sins, errors, and normal behaviors.

As each sin becomes more popular, we explain it away or simply tell ourselves that this many people cannot be wrong, and so move it into a safer category. But the categories are always changing. As the downward grade continues, more sins become errors, and more errors become normal. Want examples?

Bad people swindle others out of money. Normal people don't report all of their income, or they sue for more than damages.

Bad people get divorced. Normal people presume upon their marriages.

Bad unwed teenagers abort their babies. Normal ones proudly carry them to full term. Good ones put them up for adoption.

And so on.

In 1989, while serial killer Ted Bundy was being electrocuted in a Florida prison, the normal, law-abiding citizens were outside the prison wearing "Burn Bundy" T-shirts, or dangling stuffed animals from a miniature noose, or giving their appliances the morning off "so Ted could get his full share of juice."[6]

We cannot see that the evil which flows through all of these people runs right into *us* because we are not looking for it. We hate to see the sins we love, so we have moved them into safer categories.

A Half-Off Gospel

But, rather than awaken our society from its blissful coma, the church has **shifted from repentance to recruitment**. And by this we have christened a lower standard and a cheaper grace. Is this why the word *sin* is rarely, if ever, heard on platforms across the evangelical church?

If our message is repentance, we will speak of sin and restitution. If our goal is recruitment, we will speak of accepting Christ and joining the church. We will survey the target audience and peddle a god to meet their needs with precious little emphasis upon whether or not those needs ought to be met. We will talk about our number of converts, the forty-eight highest Sundays, and whether or not to build.

The sanctuary will replace the home or classroom as the most holy place in the church's life. And all of our energies will be poured into that one hour when everyone is together. Then we will count our attendance and compare this number with our brothers who are doing exactly the same thing.

This, of course, is the road we have taken. And so, rather than stand and preach the raw gospel of forsaking sins and bearing crosses, we call our listeners to accept Christ and naively believe they will learn the hard part later. Rather than ask them to step into the aisle and "[bear] the disgrace he bore" (Hebrews 13:13), we challenge them to make eye contact with the speaker, or repeat the prayer right in their seats. Rather than confront them with Christ on the job, we invite them to concerts and potlucks to hear the gospel in a setting less embarrassing than the present. Charles Spurgeon used to say repentance needed to be as painful as the sin was severe. But by the sound of many of our sermons today, our sin is only a misdemeanor for which the "sinner's prayer" is an out-of-court settlement.

What Is Sin?

There are about twenty words in the Bible for "sin." The most popular is *hamartia,* "to miss the mark." But in the Greek, as in most things, context is everything. And the context surrounding this missing of the mark is not merely the innocent blunder of a poor shot. It is something worse.

Sin is a problem of the will and desire. Augustine spoke of the "sin that goes before a sin," and by it meant the distorted will "to live according to man rather than according to God." In other words, our problem is not *that* we sin, but *why* we sin. This is what we call, in theology, the "sinful nature" or the "sin behind the sin."

So, while we may be known by our actions, we are always defined by our nature, in that we cannot act for very long in ways inconsistent with our nature. Jesus taught that people did bad things because they

36

were already tainted at heart (Mark 7:21-23). Or, as R. C. Sproul put it, "We are not sinners because we sin; we sin because we are sinners." The heart or mind of the person is already polluted with something that is opposed to the authority of God or the idea of surrender—something that sets itself up against the life of purity and discipline. This is what the Apostle Paul meant when he said, "Those who live according to the sinful nature have their minds set on what that nature desires, but those who live in accordance with the Spirit have their minds set on what the Spirit desires" (Romans 8:5-6).

To understand Paul's words, think of this "mind" as being governed by such things as our joys, sorrows, fears and desires. Augustine called these "the four primary passions." John Wesley added "aversions" and "hopes" to the list.

If the verse in Romans is right, our sinful acts are driven by a deeper, more significant problem, which makes our sin problem very hard to deal with. Most people will admit to committing a sin every now and then, and the more brazen admit to it with pride while they continue to sin. But the bitter pill to swallow, and the one Jesus and Paul keep shoving down our obstinate throats, is the confession that we have sinned because we are . . . well, bad people. We fear and love the wrong things. We want and avoid that which is contrary to the will of God. Our desires are perverted; our passions misdirected.

Dogs bark. Birds fly. Bees sting. Sinners sin. All for the same reason: it is their nature to do so.

But when we say our desires are perverted, what have we implied? That there is still another problem, another layer deeper. This is what Paul called our *nature* or will.

"What are desires and joys but the will in harmony with the things we desire?" asked Augustine. "And what are fears and sadness but the will in disagreement with things we abhor?"

Now slow down, and read the rest.

"The consent of the will in search for what we want is called desire; the will's consent to the enjoyment of what we desire [is called joy]; so too, fear is aversion from what we do not wish to happen, as sadness is the disagreement of the will with something that has happened against our will."[7]

The stubborn will or sinful nature is the core of the problem. The epicenter of conversion. The primary cause of all that is wrong with the world. And this is the target of holiness. Real holiness begins here and works its way outward. Anything else is just morality or integrity, or a good old-fashioned brainwashing.

Augustine said this nature, or epicenter, was ruled by immorality. Luther said it was "unbelief." Wesley said it was "self-love," which seems nearer the mark. That is, everything we do is driven by self or by, as Menninger put it, "sin with an 'I' in the middle." We may insist that sin, real sin, lies only in rude or violent people who make the evening news. But these are only the mountains of evil. Most of us hide our own evil in the valley between them. But the stratum which ties all evil together is "self." It inflicts some worse than others, but all of us suffer from it.

The infant screaming in the night for his warm bottle is more concerned with his eating than our sleeping. But this is not sin. To us, this is only "self-preservation." The two-year-old who hoards his toys and holds his breath is "learning his boundaries." This is not called sin either; it is "self-identity." The ten-year-old who ridicules the ugly duckling or fights to establish his place in the pecking order is "establishing his independence." And this is usually no sin either; it is merely the learning of a "self-image."

The rebellious teenager who wants his own car, music, morals, and curfew is "learning self-reliance," and many of his annoying customs are only normal passages into adulthood. But once again, innocent as he may be, his determination to assert his will over that of others is a grown-up version of screaming in the night. As he matures, the problem becomes more malignant. The politicking father who lives the moral life, but only because he believes good people get ahead, is driven by self-promotion. In every instance, self is at the center of our behavior. One can even "accept Christ" for selfish interests—he simply does not want to burn in hell.

The child who will not sit down, the teenager breaking the dress code, the sixth-grader smoking in the parking lot, the divorced woman turning her children against their father, the angry board member undermining his pastor, the bitter factory worker filing a counter-complaint against his supervisor . . . all of these are subtle methods of gaining our own advantage over others.

A hotel in Galveston, Texas, posted a sign in each of its rooms on the second floor, which read "NO FISHING FROM THE BALCONY." Every day, tenants stood over the railing and dangled their lines into the Gulf below. One day the management decided to take the signs down, and the fishing stopped. Here were people who fished not only when the sign said "no," but *because* the sign said "no." Yet when they returned home, they, no doubt, expected their children to share their toys and obey their teachers. These were only two symptoms of the same disease.

We cannot change the patterns of an infant, nor should we try. After all, we want them to be free and creative individuals, and a little stubbornness from them is the price we must pay. But somewhere in the later years—and usually long before we go looking for it—these, albeit natural tendencies, take an ugly turn.

Much of our talk about holiness ignores this layer of sin, preferring instead to treat only the behavior with legalism or therapy. Both efforts fail to realize that, just as the pig—after he is bathed and pampered—will waddle back to his mud hole, so will the convert return to his favorite vices (or find new ones) after every confession, until it is no longer in his *nature* to do so.

Look again at the three layers of sin we've discussed: first, the *act,* which is obvious and loathsome to anyone; but directly behind (or underneath) it is a *mind* or desire which makes the act possible (this is less obvious, but it is the real evil of the sin); finally, at the bottom of it all, is the *nature* or will of the person, whereby he chooses whom he will serve. We'll show this by using some of the most-hated sins among religious folk.

Slander   **Adultery**

Murder   **Swearing**

Boasting   **Sorrows**   **Desires**   **Theft**

Joys   **Fears**

Self-Will

This same idea can be traced in Paul's statement to the Galatians: "The sinful nature desires what is contrary to the Spirit, and the Spirit what is contrary to the sinful nature . . . so that you do not do what you want" (5:17). It is also consistent with Paul's stark admission to the Romans that, even while he was stuck in the habit of doing the bad and felt unable to do the good, it was still the good he wanted to do (Romans 7:19). His nature and desire were already changed.

Rather than crucify the apostle for his candid remarks (which has become the pastime of too many with not enough to preach about), maybe we should first back away and compare his condition to that of converts in our own churches, who still find righteousness a drag and sin a pleasure. Much of modern discipleship consists of talking "converts" into hating their sins.

The will to have it *my* way—to order my peace and affluence, to feather my own nest, to right the world according to me—first corrupts my passions and desires, then later my actions. This is the sinful nature. And the kernel underneath it all is "self."

So sin, *real* sin, is not the committing of murder, theft or adultery. It is the evil desire behind the act. It is the desire to live outside of God's presence and on our own; to put ourselves first; to make our own decisions. Whether we are taking another person's life, property or body, we are taking it for ourselves. We are exercising *our* authority over theirs. We are taking them, by power or persuasion, to serve our own interests.

In this sense, it is possible to lust sinfully even after our own wives, or covet what we already possess, or lie—even while telling the truth. For if we seek to perpetuate our own interests, even in these "harmless" pursuits, we are different only in degree, and not in kind, to the derelicts highlighted on the evening news.

This explains what the Methodist evangelist, E. Stanley Jones, meant when he confessed, "Jesus saved me from *myself* . . . the greatest salvation of all"; or what Samuel Logan Brengle's biographer understood when he described Brengle's experience of "seeing the 'I' still smeared all over his aspirations."

When the will is changed—and this is the miracle of conversion— the power of sin is broken, as Wesley taught. In the absence of selfish interests, the once-evil act has been de-fanged. Thus, Wesley could write that "all sin is a transgression of the law, but not every transgression of the law is a sin."

In responding to a *New York Times* invitation to write his answer to the question, "What is wrong with the world?", G. K. Chesterton hit the target with a three-word essay.

"Sir," he wrote, "I am."

The surest definition of sin, the full ramifications of a decent conversion, the trek toward personal holiness, begin with the discovery that evil lies in parts of my being I never knew existed. The journey begins with the passing from unconscious depravity to conscious depravity; or from sin to iniquity.

When men of old were once converted, they were converted here: inside their will and desires. They ceased to be self-directed and became God-directed at the core. The rest was the working out of their salvation with the fear and trembling that is becoming of a soul which has gazed upon the holiness of God. And their own pursuit toward holiness was the slow and painful discovery that there was more of them which needed cleansing than they first thought.

These kinds of conversions and holy passions seem so far out of reach that many give up in despair, even though they hate the alternative. That is, most people desire this kind of genuine change, but are easily intimidated into a sinkhole religion that is just enough to make them miserable, and not enough to make them happy. But the treasure is nearer than we think.

And the secret password that will take us there is "repentance."

NOTES:
[1] Associated Press, "Miami Man Beaten, Killed by Mob After Hitting Girl," *The Charlotte Observer* (July 14, 1994): p. 2A.

[2] Cited in "Guilt," *Leadership Magazine* (Fall 1993): p. 57.

[3] Karl Menninger, *Whatever Became of Sin* (New York: Bantam, 1979), p. 15.

[4] In context, Abt applied this criticism to the psyche of modern talk shows, but it is an apt summary of our culture in general, for which talk shows have become a sort of thought index. Cited by Vicki Abt and Mel Seesholtz in "The Shameless World of Phil, Sally, Oprah: Television Talk Shows & the Deconstructing of Society," *Journal of Popular Culture* (Summer 1994): p. 184.

[5] Daniel Patrick Moynihan, "Defining Deviancy Down," *American Sociological Review* (January 1993): pp. 17–30. A shorter, more interesting summary of Moynihan's arguments appears in "Moral Deregulation," *American Legion* (March 1995): p. 32.

[6] Associated Press, December 11, 1987. Cited by R. Scott Richards in *Myths the World Taught Me* (Nashville: Thos. Nelson, 1991), p. 37.

[7] Saint Augustine, *City of God,* abr. version translated by Gerald G. Walsh, Demetrius B. Zema, Grace Monahan and Daniel J. Honan (New York: Image Books, 1958), p. 303.

CHAPTER 4

HURTS SO GOOD!

The Power and the Joy of True Repentance

Can you say shibboleth?

Careful. This one could kill you.

Once, in the Old Testament, when the people of Ephraim were defeated in battle and the enemy (the Gileadites) had seized control of the river leading back to their homelands, the clever Ephraimites disguised themselves to look like Gileadites so they could get past the guards at the border.

One can easily imagine the fear and apprehension on the face of the young Ephraimite soldier as he nears the checkpoint, still limping from the wound received during the battle with the very men about to interrogate him.

"Are you an Ephraimite?" hollers one of the guards.

The soldier shakes his head and tries to look convincing. "No," he says, but his eyes give him away.

"All right then," growls the commander, "say shibboleth."

What kind of a stupid question is that? Is this all there is to it? The young soldier stops and stares into the eyes of the commander. He starts to smile.

"Sibboleth."

"Say it again."

"All right. Sibboleth."

Before he knows he has failed, he feels a stabbing pain rip through his back and into his chest. There is no air to scream. He collapses into a heap. His whole life—his laughter as a child, his mother's smile, his lovers, his first day as a soldier—races before his eyes, and then fades to black.

Game over.

Lest we forget this once-familiar story, the Bible has memorialized it in the book of Judges (chap. 12) and even reminded us that forty-two thousand others died in precisely the same manner for the same reason. Their bones form a monument to this one truth: *there are certain times in life when one simply cannot afford to be wrong.* There are passage points where we must have it all together. It is not enough to be close or sincere. One mistake, and the next sound you hear is the lid to your casket being shut and sealed.

Not surprisingly, we call these passages "shibboleths"—a password or litmus test to prove who's in and who's out.

In this sense, repentance is the shibboleth of a true conversion. It separates the genuine from the counterfeit, even though they look very much alike.

Repentance is more than an admission of guilt. It is a well-aimed missile into the heart of our sinful nature.

It is neither sorrow without change, nor change without sorrow. It is sorrow with *intent to change.*

It is unconditional surrender. Kneeling down inside. The Bible associates it with . . .

- an acknowledgment of guilt and personal responsibility (1 Kings 8:47);
- the slaughter of pride (2 Chronicles 32:26);
- the despising of oneself (Job 42:6);
- humility under correction (Jeremiah 5:3);
- deep sorrow over the wrong we have done (Jeremiah 31:19);
- the renunciation of past sins (Ezekiel 14:6; Jonah 3:8);
- getting a new heart and spirit (Ezekiel 18:31; 36:26).

Repentance is vastly underestimated today by people on opposite ends of the spectrum. First, it is rejected by pagans who refuse to change their darkened minds or to worship anything besides their bellies. But it is also ignored by those in holiness traditions who have moved everything resembling change or reformation into the "entire sanctification" column. These misguided people allow "Christians" to get away with murder in the name of "carnality," and then hang on to their own sins for years. A good many of them are wrestling what they should surrender, or resting when they should feel themselves perturbed.

But true repentance is not the first step toward salvation. It *is* salvation. In the Old Testament, "repentance," or *nacham,* is associated with both emotion (Genesis 6:7) and resolve (Exodus 13:17). One scholar has called it an "admission of wrongdoing followed by grief and leading to a wiser course."[1] In the New Testament, "repentance" *(metanoia)* is used to describe the changing of one's mind.

In true repentance, then, the seeker changes his mind, not only about God, but about himself and his sin. This involves not only a turning away from sin, but a turning toward God with humility and conviction. So repentance is a ramp which determines the trajectory my Christian life will take. The faith which follows, and whether or not I enjoy it, will depend on the "takeoff." This is why the Bible's formula for conversion—"repent and believe the good news" (Mark 1:15)—is much simpler than ours. Early Christians expected more from their repentance . . . and got it.

But things have changed. If you believe the polls, a conversion experience makes little or no difference as to whether or not a person believes in absolute truth, or that the purpose of life is enjoyment, or that it is better to get even than mad, or that his first responsibility in life is to himself.[2]

The Pauline epistles just went out the window.

The top three values of the secular man are family, health and time. The top three values of the "born-again Christian" are family, health and religion.[3] Yet, Jesus talked about hating one's mother and father (Luke 14:26), and even one's own life (John 12:25), in order to be His disciple. So why is religion third?

Today's "converts" don't even attend church. According to research from 1991, the United Methodists needed 25 converts to add a single person to their most popular service. The Wesleyan Church was not much better, with a ratio of 21 to 1. The Assemblies of God had a ratio of 8 to 1. The United Brethren in Christ, 7 to 1. And the Church of God (Anderson), 6 to 1. Many other denominations report thousands of conversions, all the while posting huge losses in their most popular service.[4]

We would not make worship attendance the shibboleth of true repentance. But if modern repentance does not affect our beliefs, values, or desire to fellowship with other believers, then what does it affect? What got converted? From what were we saved? Where is the *metanoia?*

Pseudo-conversions fill our churches and our leadership, and this has put us in an awkward predicament. The very minds we once only tolerated, we have come to embrace, even depend upon to run committees, teach classes, and fill pulpits. Could it be that we actually ordain some who will be turned away from heaven because they cannot say "shibboleth"?

Now is a pretty good time to determine what exactly is meant by the call to "repent . . . [and] produce fruit in keeping with repentance" (Matthew 3:2, 8). It is a question addressed by many in the past, but few, if any, in today's "judge not" society. Yet, the reason so many never pursue holiness in their Christian lives is that they were (shall we say it?) *never truly converted* in the first place. Not everyone who repents is repentant. Judas wasn't (see Matthew 27:3).

So, let's look at a few contrasts between true and false repentance.

1. True repentance is motivated by inner conviction.
False repentance is motivated by outer pressure.

When a man is truly sorry for his sins, he does not wait for the rent to come due, nor the court to settle, nor the media to find out. He is driven by conviction and not pressure.

There are some who seem ready to repent as a way to fix their troubled lives, yet too often they grieve only the sins of the present crisis, and no more. So, when the pressure is off, their repentance is over. Only *this* is not true repentance. It is crisis management.

Others simply want to avoid hell, and so they surrender any sins they believe will send them there. *This* is not repentance either. It is death insurance.

But there is a kind of repentance which heads to the temple when no one else is looking, and cries, "God have mercy on me, a sinner" (Luke 18:13). It is motivated by the conviction that one has offended a holy God and is willing to do anything to reconcile. Tears, confessions, and altar calls do not deter the man thus motivated. He may experience any of these or none, but his compulsion is from within, and his audience is in heaven. He is not thinking of anything else.

2. True repentance abhors sin.
False repentance minimizes sin.

"Unrepentant sinners may look at sin and see that it will ruin them, knowing God will punish them for it, but the sin itself appears desirable to them," noted Charles Finney. "If their sin could end in happiness, they never would think of abandoning it."[5]

This is false repentance. It will gloss over the transgression, or excuse it, or call it something else. False repentance cannot understand why the prosecution makes so much of sin. This is because it does not hate sin itself, only the grief or inconvenience which follows.

True repentance is to change our minds about many things, beginning with our love for sin itself. We regret the past. We do not believe sin was fun while it lasted, and those who conspire to sin today and repent for it later do not have true repentance in mind.

This does not mean we will never sin again. It only means my "want-to" has been changed, and the good which I strive to do will be "the good I *want* to do," and the evil I resist will be "the evil I *do not want* to do" (Romans 7:19, italics added).

3. True repentance accepts the consequences. False repentance seeks to avoid them.

There are many today who confess the crime but resist the consequence—as though confession suspends the law of reaping what you sow.

When televangelist Jimmy Swaggart confessed his sin of pornography, his real problem (self-worship) surfaced later when he refused to submit to the discipline of his denomination. It could be that whatever prompted him to defy authority also led him to hire a prostitute to perform obscene acts for him. But, even if it didn't, this kind of repentance more resembles the sorrow of Saul, who said, "I have sinned. But please honor me before the elders of my people" (1 Samuel 15:30a); or that of Simon the Sorcerer, who pleaded with Peter, "Pray to the Lord for me so that nothing you have said may happen to me" (Acts 8:24).

False repentance minimizes the consequences and usually underestimates the agony and the time necessary to heal. It wants to forget and move on. It circumvents the restoration process by hurrying it.

The truly penitent prodigal is willing to return as a servant and not as a son. He remembers, as did the dying thief, that God owes him nothing, for God has done nothing wrong, but realizes that he is "getting what [his] deeds deserve" (Luke 23:41). He says, with the people of Judah, "The LORD Almighty has done to us what our ways and practices deserve" (Zechariah 1:6). He accepts this as his lot.

Interestingly, even after Jonah preached and the Ninevites repented, they still did not presume upon the forgiveness of God. "Who knows?"

said their king when he commanded his subjects to repent. "God may yet relent and . . . turn from his fierce anger so that we will not perish" (Jonah 3:9). The implication here, of course, is that God *may not* turn from His anger and forgive them. But even this grim prospect does not deter them from repenting.

For it is not hell the penitent heart fears most, but the disfavor of God. Even so, we must get past the idea that "repentance" is only the lever that opens the prison of blame and consequence.

4. True repentance is changed behavior.
False repentance is cyclical confession.

There's an important distinction between "you're right" and "I'm wrong." The first is only a confession. When a man confesses, he merely agrees with God—which never impresses God, since He has known He is right all along. But to confess is not to change, nor even to desire it.

To those who only confess, "virtue consists in confessing sins, not in avoiding them," wrote William Mavis, "and to the degree that this lessens the impulse for righteous living, it may be a demonic substitute."

It is here that one remembers the warning of humorist Josh Billings: "The hardest sinner of all is one who spends half of his time sinning and the other half repenting."

We will be accused of being legalistic, but we must insist that, while faith alone is the only requirement for salvation, that very faith may be proven by its willingness to seek and desire change. J. I. Packer simply called it "a settled refusal to set any limit to the claims [Christ] will make on our lives." Even with stubborn habits and learned behaviors, the genuine seeker sets in motion the very disciplines he knows will destroy the stronghold of sin in his life. Associations are surrendered, schedules changed, relationships severed, restitutions made—all in order to reconcile with God.

5. True repentance begs forgiveness.
False repentance promises to do better.

True repentance is about forgiveness and restoration, first with God—whose laws alone we have broken—and then with any others we may have offended. It is not about restoring old friendships, healing memories, or taking responsibility for one's mistakes. It is not the gate to wholeness, but holiness.

We may admit to our problems. We may vow to start this or stop that. We may humbly accept any consequences we have coming. But, until we have thrown ourselves at the mercy of God, we have done something other than repent. For repentance is a *spiritual* exercise. It is bowing the knee to an audience of One.

It is not acknowledging only our sin, but also our complete helplessness to do anything about it. Wesley wrote, "We must cast away all confidence in our own righteousness, or we cannot have a true confidence in His; until we are delivered [through repentance] from trusting in anything we can do, we cannot thoroughly trust in what He has done and suffered."[6]

6. True repentance is a habit.
False repentance is a debut.

"The individual who truly repents," wrote Finney, "does not close his eyes to the tendencies of sin." So it is that Martin Luther began his Ninety-Five Theses on this very premise: that "when our Lord and Master, Jesus Christ, said 'repent,' He called for the entire life of believers to be one of penitence."

The deceived stop searching for their sin the moment they believe they are forgiven. To them, repentance is only the turnstile into the kingdom of heaven—something to be left at the gate once they are safely inside. This is evident from the reluctance of many Christians to confess anything they do as a "sin." Yet, if these people repented long ago like they confess today (that is, if they *then* denied their sinfulness like they *now* deny their failures), one is left to wonder at the sincerity of their conversion in the first place.

In truth, the search for sin in our lives has only begun the day we are converted. And each time we find it, we repent of it, and the process continues. Those growing in holiness will tell you that perpetual self-examination plays as big a part in their daily walk as it did in their initial conversion. For it is the discipline of contrition, and not the feigning of perfection, which leads to the sanctification of the sinner.

The Joy of Repentance

So, true repentance is not the hurry-up apology we pretend. But neither is it a pounding into the ground. It is a radical surgery. But it is not an execution. That is, it hurts. But it hurts good.

This is the side of repentance we seldom hear about. So what are the benefits?

For starters, when we repent, we feel a relief in knowing **we have come nearer to what really ails us.** No one looks forward to surgery, but when surgery is necessary, the patient at least wants the assurance that the surgeon knows exactly what he is after. It is painful, to be sure, but less painful than the ongoing saga of not knowing what's wrong with us. Even when we can't cure it, we want to hear that the disease has been given a name.

Of course, there are those who refuse to see the doctor for fear of what he might find. They would rather *imagine* they are going to die than hear it for sure. But this is an idiot's delight.

There is a spiritual analogy here. Rather than face the "mandatory confrontation between themselves and Christ," as philosopher Blaise Pascal called it, there are some who occupy themselves with things that are really quite trivial, but still less painful than the sting of repentance. They would rather *feel* like they are sinful than know it for sure. But this is only as far as the analogy goes, for God has promised that the wounding we dread will be the scar we need, and that, if we will stick with it, we will always be healed in the end. For true repentance exposes the very problem God is after, and He is capable of removing it. But He does not yank it out of us.

So, if you are one who hates the disease and fears the physician—that is, if you're tired of sin and want to confess it, but are still afraid that God will upset too many other things in the process—it is your *fear* that you should surrender and not merely your vices. Once you do, you will have driven a stake into the heart of your unbelief. The rest of your problems will very soon after fade away.

Another advantage to repentance is that **it removes guilt.** As surely as guilt provokes repentance, repentance relieves guilt. Maybe this is why so many doubt their salvation.

I have counseled many who grew up under a truckload of rules, and who conscientiously confessed to each one, but never have felt their sins forgiven. Yet, if you ask them specifically what they have done wrong, they can hardly tell you. They believe they are sinners, but do not know why. They do not remember what, exactly, God forgave. Thus, their salvation was more of a general absolution for their (still unacknowledged) sins.

This is not poor self-esteem. This is a spiritual problem. Could it be that the conversion experience of these people was less a repentance and more an apology? Could it be that they sought deliverance from guilt in general and not sin in particular?

As a rule, we might say that God will heal what we reveal in our repentance, or that the cleansing is only as deep as the confession. It was only after Isaiah's confession ("I am a man of unclean lips" [Isaiah 6:5]) that his sin was forgiven. And then only concerning the very part of him for which he confessed, for the live coal from the altar was touched against his *lips*. With this, his "guilt [was] taken away and [his] sin atoned for" (Isaiah 6:7). Had Isaiah's confession been less specific, the story may have ended quite differently.

Likewise, if we confess to breaking a rule, the guilt of the transgression is taken away. But the guilt of sinful passions underneath—which made the rule a nuisance and the breaking of it a pleasure, and which just about guarantees that it will happen again—all goes unaffected. So maybe it isn't really forgiveness the poor soul desires, but cleansing. And only repentance can help that.

There is one more real benefit and joy to the life of repentance: **it marks a new beginning.**

Back to Isaiah. I have often wondered whether the prophet spoke with a lisp from that day forward, since the live coal was applied to his "unclean lips." If he did, he must have worn it with a certain fondness, for the day he was scarred was the day he received his calling. Even as Jacob's limp would remind him of the night his name was changed, the scar on Isaiah's lip would remind him of the day his sin was purged and his mission began. From that day forward, whenever he spoke, it would be over the scar received in the Temple.

There are those who would receive a mission gladly, were it not for the wounding just before. But, first things first. And, as surely as sin has its consequences, repentance does, too. It is the joy of guilt acknowledged and guilt expunged; the surprise of power surrendered and power received.

The German theologian, Helmut Thielicke, has an interesting theory as to why the prodigal son returned, and it touches on the very point I have just made.

The thing that raised him up was not the weariness with the far country, nor was it the fear of the void. . . . No, what gave him new initiative was recalling that his father's house was open to him, that a waiting candle burned in the window, and that he would be met by one who loved him and would recognize the failure, in all his rags, as his own flesh and blood.[7]

Thielicke says, "Repentance is, therefore, not the negation of what we have behind us. It is the joyous breakthrough to what we have *before* us" (italics in original). And what we have before us is a life "of righteousness, peace and joy in the Holy Spirit" (Romans 14:17b). For through our repentance, the die has already been cast for a lifestyle of faith, submission and holiness.

Sanctification will come later; but when it comes, it will not be because we decided to push our religion to the next level or finally to commit ourselves. As we shall see, our sanctification will be the logical conclusion to our conversion. For in it, we were "predestined to be conformed" to Christ's image (Romans 8:29). He will not rest, and neither will we, until we are.

NOTES:
[1] Robert B. Girdlestone, *Synonyms of the Old Testament* (Grand Rapids: Eerdmans, 1897), p. 89.

[2] George Barna, *What Americans Believe* (Ventura: Regal, 1991), pp. 85, 94, 103, 88.

[3] Ibid., p. 157.

[4] I conducted this research myself by soliciting the statistics of the number of conversions and the amount of increase in the most popular service. While this simple formula does not allow for deaths and membership transfers, these are often offset by the number of births and membership-in transfers which increase the attendance without conversions.

[5] Charles G. Finney, *Principles of Salvation,* comp. by Louis Gifford Parkhurst, Jr. (Minneapolis: Bethany House, 1989), p. 44.

[6] John Wesley, *A Compound of Wesley's Theology,* ed. by Robert W. Burtner and Robert E. Chiles (New York: Abingdon, 1954), pp. 155–56.

[7] Helmut Thielicke, *Being a Christian When the Chips Are Down*, trans. by H. George Anderson (London: Fort Press & Wm. Collins Sons, 1979), p. 44.

CHAPTER 5

FIRST-CLASS CONVERSIONS

Salvation Through the Spectacles of Holiness

I might win ten million dollars.

Here's how: I received a light brown envelope in the mail the other day with Ed McMahon's picture on it. He said,

"Steven L. DeNeff."

How does he know me?

Then he said,

"You could win $10 million from the Publisher's Clearinghouse Sweepstakes."

I know that everybody gets one of these, but *mine* had "FINAL DRAWING" stamped on the envelope, and when I opened it, Mr. McMahon said he wanted to hand *me* the check personally. Beat that!

Now wait. Before you try to sell me a bridge in Brooklyn, you should know I didn't really believe all of that stuff. Like you, I am despairingly aware that millions of people get the same letter from Ed; that their names are laser-printed onto the letterhead just like mine was; that "final drawing" means there's only one, and it hasn't happened yet; and that all of this means I don't have the slightest chance of winning.

So I haven't spent the money yet. In fact, my chances are even slimmer now that I threw the offer away.

Nevertheless, "junk mail," as we call it, is a multi-billion-dollar business, soliciting thousands of requests from people who didn't know they needed something until they went to the mailbox (as Os Guinness remarked, "All they love is need"). Advertising is a ten-million-dollar business every day in the United States, and much of it goes for junk mail. The idea is to saturate the area with your advertisement, on the assumption that a fraction of the addressees will respond, and a fraction of *that* number will buy your product. It's a one-time, generic invitation to all the people in hopes that a few will take the bait. Fishermen call it "trolling": using one lure for every fish in the sea.

Junk-Mail Evangelism

It occurs to me that maybe we have come to preach a kind of "junk-mail evangelism" in the "land of opportunity." Ever since the triumph of Arminianism in the early nineteenth century, we have defaulted into a belief that God has marketed His gospel the way Publisher's Clearinghouse markets periodicals: He has made a product, and now anyone interested can come and get it.

"Come to me, all you who are weary and burdened, and I will give you rest," goes the advertising jingle of busy evangelists who use the words of Jesus to package their product into four spiritual laws. It's a one-time, generic invitation to all people, in hopes that a few will take the bait. We believe that God has acted once in history, and now the rest is up to us.

And if this is not true, then why do we often pay more attention to the package of our message, than to the content of it? Why do we speak of "accepting" Christ—a term that is foreign to Scripture (in which Christ accepts us), but is common to the textbooks of marketing? Why do books about "closing the sale" or "marketing the church" (with no apologies from their authors) clutter the bestseller shelves of our local Christian bookstores? Why is there more interest in soul winning than in intercessory prayer, as though a man's conversion depended on an articulate presentation of the gospel? And why do we speak of "attracting" someone to the church before we evangelize them?

If we truly believe that in salvation God gives *himself* to the individual and that the individual does not merely respond to a generic offer given to the whole world at once, then why do we hornswoggle people into the church and onto the rolls?

The truth is that the gospel of Christ may be an equal opportunity, but it is not an indiscriminate one, and it is surely not self-serve. God must convict the individual, or he cannot repent (see 2 Timothy 2:25). He must know the individual, or she cannot be saved (see Matthew 7:23). God must guide the individual, or he cannot know the truth (see John 16:13). We believe in free will. But do we believe in *this?*

I have had my share of junk mail (nine pieces one day), and I have noticed a parallel between the junk-mail mentality and the current misbeliefs we have about conversion. Because we have adapted ourselves to a junk-mail mentality, we often misunderstand the power and the glory and the exceeding high call of the gospel upon our lives. And all of this has to do with holiness. For it is in conversion that our holiness is born.

Our Peculiarity

The Myth: I was not chosen—I chose!
The Truth: God chose us.

As we already have pointed out, our modern version of grace holds that God circulated the call of salvation to the whole world at once. Everybody got the same invitation, at the same time, and in identical packages. And it is the job of the evangelist to keep these packages (i.e., the plan of salvation) moving around so everyone has a chance to respond. This is our modern version of a generic, bulk rate, brown-enveloped offer from God.

"For God so loved the world," we tell ourselves (John 3:16), and assume that it is personal because of our association with the world.

"You're in the world," I have assured some, "so you count."

It may be true. But, for one reason or another (whether pride or low self-esteem), it isn't very convincing. And why should it be? All of this sounds so uncertain. It weakens the meaning of "the power of God unto salvation" (Romans 1:16 KJV), and it reduces God to an advertiser, and men to mere consumers.

In this scheme of things, our conversion is more of a *want* than a *need*. And worse, it puts the emphasis of conversion, and the credit for the blessings which follow, onto the man who responded, rather than onto God who offered in the first place. What separates the Christian from all others is not the invitation (since everybody got one), but that *he* has taken full responsibility for himself and developed the good sense to go after it.

He prayed.

He consecrated himself.

He searched his heart, then played the man and repented.

The others didn't. So he deserves what he gets, and they deserve what they get. But whatever happened to grace?[1]

Junk-Mail Consumers

It is fairly simple to detect which people (or if we ourselves) have begun to believe in junk-mail conversion.

1. They have a compulsion to make everything "happen" in their Christian lives.

They put themselves down for all they have *not* achieved, and constantly compare themselves to others who are doing much better. To them, holiness is a long, arduous task, and they are responsible for carrying it out alone. And when their lives unravel (as those of self-made Christians usually do), it is always because *they* did not consecrate themselves, or *they* did not really mean it when they did, or *they* have not had their devotions lately, or *they* have angered the gods, or . . .

John Wesley warned us that the Devil "often dampens the joy we should otherwise feel in what we have already attained, by a perverse representation of what we have not attained . . . so that we cannot rejoice in what we have because there is more which we have not." He added that this temptation is greatest among those with the most intensity toward holiness. In chapter eight, we will tackle specifically this temptation to hurry.

2. They have a low appreciation for the work of God in their salvation.

They have taken the "amazing" out of grace. They speak only of hard work and spiritual disciplines in their testimonies. They look past the tremendous advantage the Holy Spirit brings into a person's life.

3. They ignore the "personality" of God.

To them, God is the sum total of a higher law, or the apex of all moral reasoning; He is an absolute, albeit far-removed, version of purity and perfection. These people are always reasoning themselves or discipling themselves closer to God, much like a mountain climber would scale the cold, stony faces of Mount Rushmore. To these people, God is the unseen advertiser behind the junk-mail offer of grace to any and every one who asks for it. They secretly hope He will one day hand them the check personally, but they want to be realistic, too.

4. They are often unsure of their salvation.

Since their conversion was largely their own idea, God's Spirit does not bear witness to their spirit, because God's Spirit very likely wasn't there when they were "saved." They likely received Christ when He was not offered to them. They jumped too soon.

Now all of this is wrong, as Paul tries to point out in his epistles. For if the apostle was right, God "chose us in him before the creation of the world to be holy and blameless in his sight. . . . [and] to be adopted as his sons through Jesus Christ. . . . in order that we . . . might be for the praise of his glory" (Ephesians 1:4-5, 12). That's the gist of Paul's theology on the matter.

The original language of these verses indicates that all of this happened at one particular time, and was the result of God's own decision. "God picked us out for himself," the Greek scholar, J. H. Thayer, translates these verses. Nearly every other scholar agrees. And this is consistent with God's actions elsewhere in Scripture, as well.

To Israel, He said, "The LORD your God has chosen you out of all the peoples on the face of the earth to be his people, his treasured possession" (Deuteronomy 7:6b).

Through Jeremiah, He promised to "choose . . . one from a town and two from a clan" (Jeremiah 3:14).

Through Haggai, He vowed to His servant, Zerubbabel, ". . . I will make you like my signet ring, for I have chosen you . . ." (Haggai 2:23).

And who can forget His charge to the persecuted believers of the first century: "But you are a chosen people, a royal priesthood, a holy nation, a people belonging to God" (1 Peter 2:9a).

Anyone who ever stood in line as a child, and waited to be picked by a team captain, knows the fear and rejection of being the last one chosen. But the believer can take stock in the fact that God chose him and called him by name. This person will not speak of battles fought, nor habits broken, nor disciplines learned. He will speak of that day when God's Spirit moved over his own spirit, and started a holy fire inside him which the believer himself has only nourished.

This person was not drafted by the lotto, nor flushed by some form of mass evangelism. He was selected by God, in the same way a husband of the first century selected his wife: as an act of love and desire. This person has been converted or sanctified because Christ revealed the Father to him (see Matthew 11:27), and because the Spirit moved on him like He did not move on others in the room that day. There was a window of opportunity, and he was paying attention.

He needed to stay alert. He needed to repent. And he needed to exercise his faith. But he is humbled by the fact that God used a first-class invitation of the one gospel, and delivered it personally in a language he could understand, and with offers he would need, expressions he would recognize, and love he could interpret . . . and all during a time when he could listen. This is no do-it-yourself religion. This is grace. Prevenient grace. This is election. And *this* is the gospel.[2]

Destiny

The Myth: The gospel is a high-response, low-demand invitation.
The truth: God is more concerned with how far we go, than with how many are going.

The second characteristic of modern, junk-mail conversion is that it grossly underestimates the high call of our initial salvation. For in it, we were predestined to a life of holy living, or we were never truly saved.

"He chose us in him . . . to be holy and blameless in His sight" (Ephesians 1:4), said Paul. And again, "Those God foreknew, he also predestined to be conformed to the likeness of his Son" (Romans 8:29). In fact, the whole doctrine of predestination has less to do with *who goes to heaven,* than with *the character of those who are going.*

Predestination implies that the destiny of our faith is holiness, just as matrimony implies that the destiny of our engagement is love. Like marriage, our salvation is not just a legal contract in which we juggle the books of heaven. It is a bond of union between ourselves and Christ, or it is a very bad marriage.

Nevertheless, because we believe in junk-mail conversion, **we believe we can take more of salvation if we want it, or less if we don't.** My Publisher's Clearinghouse letter says I can double the value of their offer if I will only subscribe to a dozen periodicals at drastically reduced prices. But, either way, whether I want the extras or only the ten million dollars, I am in the drawing and the choice is always mine.

In similar fashion, it is no wonder that those who confuse "grace accepted" with "grace offered" also treat holiness as though it were some sort of addendum to their conversion. I believe this lies at the root of all the misunderstanding today over sanctification. We believe, as any consumer would, that we can take God's original offer as far as we want it to go. If we want the deluxe, limited edition of Christianity, we will be saved *and* sanctified. But if we want to avoid the high cost and upkeep, we may settle for the standard model. Either way, we assume the choice is ours.

Well, it isn't.

Being chosen always carries with it the idea of separation, which is also the meaning of holiness. Throughout the Bible, people, places and things are said to be "chosen" when they are separated from the ordinary for the glory of God (see 2 Timothy 2:20-21).

Israel is said to be chosen from among other nations, to be the people of God. This is why they are called a "holy nation," and were given the Law, which is peculiar to them (see Romans 9:4). During the Passover feast, the paschal lamb was said to be chosen from among the others, because it was "without defect" (Exodus 12:5). The tribe of Levi was separated from all other tribes to be the priests of God. Certain people were chosen, then separated from the rest of their people, to be patriarchs and kings. Jerusalem is said to be chosen from among all other cities, to be the city of God. In the Gospels, James and John were chosen by God to be disciples, and they left the others still in the boat (see Mark 1:20). In the early church, Matthias was chosen by a peculiar method of casting lots, and was separated from Joseph, who was not chosen.

"You did not choose me, but I chose you . . ." Jesus told His disciples, and then went on to explain the idea of separation: ". . . I have chosen you out of the world . . ." (John 15:16, 19).

The plain truth of Scripture is that none are chosen who are not also predestined to be conformed to the likeness of Christ. Sanctification is not "part two" of the gospel. It is the gospel itself, for Christ will have none who will not be holy.

Moreover, like good consumers who know they are always right, **we believe the offers for salvation and sanctification are forever open.** Since the junk-mail convert believes his salvation was the result of opportunity seized, rather than opportunity offered, he thinks he can respond whenever he is good and ready, and that high-pressure sermons which offer salvation "for a limited time only" are really false advertising, because God, like any junk-mail advertiser, is willing to peddle His gospel and His holiness whenever He can, and to whomever will buy it.

Wrong again!

As I will say later, we cannot call ourselves sane nor Christian if we foolishly believe we may accept Christ (salvation) or may consecrate ourselves (sanctification) whenever we want to. We can't. Wesley taught that whosoever will may come . . . but not whenever he wants.[3] Scripture bears the same record.

Therefore, we must never assume we can sow our wild oats in the teenage years because the Spirit of God patiently understands our adolescent rebellion and will be kind enough to offer again later. Maybe He won't. We must never presume to "give it some thought" when we are convicted by the truth, and then to table the matter indefinitely, as though Christ will wait forever with His hat in His hand.

We have it all backwards. For who's to say that, even after we are admitted into heaven, we will not one day be sat down—one at a time— and reminded of the numberless opportunities we had to receive a greater measure of godliness on earth, but missed because we simply were not paying attention? What if it is not our habits and excesses, but our lost opportunities which will most convict us on that day? Could this be the only agony in heaven? Could it be that those who took a seat, once they were saved, and rested while they waited for time on earth to run out, will find themselves as uncomfortable as any sinner on the day they stand before Holiness? After all, like the sinner, these nominal souls have stopped the grace of God. They will find that heaven is less interested in populating itself than in determining the virtue of anyone who enters it (see Revelation 21:27).

Our Rights and Privileges

The Myth: We are consumers of the gospel.
The Truth: We are children of God.
The third characteristic of modern junk-mail conversion is that it fails to comprehend the meaning of sonship, which is one of the great themes of the New Testament.
"What is a Christian?" writes J. I. Packer. "The question can be answered in many ways, but the richest answer I know is that a Christian is one who has God for his Father."
To appreciate this, we need only to survey other religions of the world and see how the gods work to keep their subjects at bay. Even in the Old Testament, it was rare for any Hebrew to call God his Father, and it was unthinkable to call himself a son of God.[4] And so, by the time Jesus finished His Sermon on the Mount, the theologians were picking themselves off the grassy slopes, for, in Matthew's account, Jesus refers to God as our "Father" seventeen times in one afternoon, and even adds that we "may be sons of [our] Father in heaven" (Matthew 5:45a).
In our conversion, Jesus offers us a relationship with God that is peculiar to Christianity alone. Other religions may claim that the gods favor some and not others, and most religions will demand some level of piety from their followers. But only Christianity brings us into the realm of a family, as the offspring of God, and after the lineage of those great names in our past we have come to call our "brothers" and "sisters." The joint-heir status we enjoy with Christ, and the "Abba Father" we cry to God are the very heart and soul of what it means to be chosen.
And it is here that a junk-mail mentality will let us down. By putting the emphasis of our conversion squarely upon our own shoulders, modern evangelism invites us into a network of beliefs, rather than into the home of a loving Father, and thus do we become better theologians than sons. We simply learn the system that saved us.
My junk-mail solicitors do not want to know me. They want to recruit me. They have my address, but they want my business. And that is all they want. So I could never approach them with sad prospects like

a broken marriage or a chapter eleven bankruptcy. They wouldn't care. My relationship with them—and this is important—is strictly utilitarian. No small talk. Just name, address, item number, and amount due. And will that be cash or credit, sir? If I am not ordering something, we have nothing to talk about. And I have just described the prayer life of too many Christians.

One tragic casualty of junk-mail conversion is that **it renders the relationship one has with God as totally utilitarian.** Too many people today are not Christians "for the praise of his glory" (Ephesians 1:12), but to save themselves from a worse alternative. But, once again, the concept of choseness implies a relationship and not merely an arbitration with God. Prayers become two-sided. Conversations are honest. Time together is presumed. Presence is enjoyed. Imperfections are overlooked in deference to love and acceptance. Choseness implies holiness. And holiness means we can *know* God, and not just keep His commandments. One is an affinity. The other is a contract.

A host of Old Testament references point to the fact that God "chose" His people, in order to have a relationship with them that was peculiar from His relationship with anyone else. So, through conversion, God has chosen us to be children . . . even heirs of God. And for this purpose, He has placed a mighty seal inside us to guarantee our maturity. This seal is the Holy Spirit, who is the love of our affair with God.

It is significant that Paul should refer to our salvation as "the adoption of children" (Ephesians 1:5 KJV); and John should insist that "we should be called children of God" (1 John 3:1). For the concept of adoption during the early centuries is very parallel with our call to sanctification. The purpose of adoption in the New Testament was not only to perpetuate the family name (which was the Roman custom), but also to confer the rights and privileges of the family onto the adopted (which was the Jewish custom).

So God is not a producer who dispenses grace and holiness to those consumers who want it. He is more of a Father who adopts only those orphans desperate enough to need it. And He does so in order to enter a relationship with them. For God will have no acquaintances in heaven. He will have only sons and daughters.

Now, if we are His children, we must one day bear the image of the Father. And if we do not, then we were not born after the Spirit, but after the flesh (whether it be in the form of a sermon or a man). And if we are born after the Spirit, we will have our Father's eyes, voice, heart, and peculiar way of responding to this or that situation. We will have His smile, and eventually, His temperament and demeanor. Give us time, and we will be a "spittin' image" of Him, whose image has been planted firmly in us, because—unlike consumers—we know we are never the product of things we consume, but of whatever consumes us.

A friend of mine crossed the dirt road one snowy Michigan morning to visit awhile with her neighbor and his two-year-old son as they shoveled their driveway together. After a brief conversation with the man about his new job, my friend bent over and asked the little boy, who was still clutching his plastic shovel, "And what do you want to be when you grow up?"

Without any hesitation, the two-year-old grabbed his father's knee, looked up at the giant of a man, and blurted, "I wanna be just like my daddy!"

It really isn't much more sophisticated than that. To be chosen by God is to be born by His Spirit. Not because I have responded to a bulk-rate, brown-enveloped, one-size-fits-all gospel, but because God has targeted me for salvation, and, through my repentance and faith, He has delivered it . . . first class!

To be chosen by God is to be the object of His love. It is to link up with a long chain of godly men and women, from Abraham to the present, and in all countries of the world, whose destiny is holiness. It is to comprehend that, as the very offspring of God, I am singled out to bear His name and to wear His image . . . "for the praise of His glory."

And *that* is worth more than ten million dollars!

NOTES:
[1] I am not espousing the Calvinist view of predestination. I am only trying to reestablish the biblical order of God's offer and our response. The whole of Scripture testifies to our utter dependence upon God for salvation. We cannot accept what God does not first offer. We cannot obey a conscience which He has not first planted within us. We cannot "work out" what He has never first "worked in" (see Philippians 2:12-13). We cannot pray unless He has first desired to hear us, and has placed within us the good desire to be heard. Wesley reminded us that "the very first motion of good is from above, as well as the power which conducts it to the end," and that "it is God that not only infuses every good desire, but that accompanies it and follows it, else it vanishes away" (*On Working Out Your Own Salvation*, Works, Vol. VI, [London: WM Book Room, p. 509]). Of course, even after God has done this, we still must respond with an effort and a cooperation of our own. Even Augustine (generally considered a Predestinarian) said, "He that made us without ourselves, will not save us without ourselves."

[2] What some have called 'natural conscience,' John Wesley termed a "preventing [or prevenient] grace." This includes the general discretion between good and evil, the aspirations to be more or better than we currently are, the innate sense of guilt, or the idea that there is a day of reckoning ahead. These are not the private possessions of a few well-disciplined men. They are the general property of sinner and saint, civilized and barbarian, slave and free, educated and ignorant alike. They are a kind of *light that lighteth every man*. The miracle is that God's Spirit moves with those strong impressions, more at some times than others, and with varying degrees within each person. The fundamental distinction between

Calvinism and Wesleyanism here is that, unlike Calvinists, Wesleyans do not believe that these impressions are confined to a few (termed "absolute predestination"), or that they are necessarily irresistible (termed "irresistible grace") once they are perceived. Instead, the cooperation of man in his own salvation means that conversion is not the coup d'etat of grace, but the surrender of a soul that has felt itself alone with God. In this sense, we are elected from among those who have ignored the Spirit up to this time or who have worked hard to suppress these impressions. For a concise summary of these distinctions, see Wesley's "What Is an Arminian?"

[3] This is a summary of Wesley's teaching on prevenient grace. Wesley wrote, "To say every man can believe to justification or sanctification *when* he will is contrary to plain matter of fact. Everyone can confute it by his own experience. And yet if you deny that every man can believe *if* he will, you run full into absolute decree. How will you untie this knot? I apprehend very easily. That every man may believe if he will I earnestly maintain, and yet that he can believe when he will I totally deny. But there will always be something in the matter which we cannot well comprehend or explain." *The Letters of John Wesley*, ed. by John Telford, (London; Epworth Press, 1931), p. 287. It is no wonder Wesley considered himself "a hair's breadth from Calvinism."

[4] For an interesting study of the irony of Jesus' use of "Father" to describe God, see Joachim Jeremias's *The Prayers of Jesus* (Great Britain: Robt. Cunningham & Sons, 1967), pp. 29–65.

CHAPTER 6

THE HEART OF THE MATTER

What is Entire Sanctification?

Throughout history, man has felt compelled, not only to have his religion, but to excel in it. He wants it to be more than average. Whatever your religion, if you truly understand it, you know it is selling you more than heaven. And it wants more than your tithe and attendance in return. Let it in, and it will push itself around until it owns and operates every square inch of your life. Tell me your religion, and I will tell you where you will be in ten years. It is a mighty force, an inner drive that pulls literally *everything* in its wake. Anything less is a fascination—a harmless set of opinions.

One might argue that the moment a belief becomes a religion, it has entered the realm of the dangerous. For religion—by its very insistence that all of life stems from the sacred—is a very possessive thing, and nearly always breeds the fanatical. In that sense, *only* religion can do this. For the only time one is fanatical about anything—whether sports, politics, music, computers or antiques—is the time he has converted his fascination into a religion, complete with its worship, sins and sacrifices.

God as a Hobby

The irony is that, while the Christian dons his faith as the "one true religion," his God possesses none of the holy terror that makes impositions upon the other gods of the world. The modern god is so nice, he'll take whatever we can afford to give him: a two-bit tithe, an hour or two every Sunday, and grace before meals. He wants us to like him and to join his religion. He is not particularly interested in what happens after that. Thus, the god of many Christians today is no God at all. He is a hobby. And his hot-tub religion has become a laughingstock to the primitive peoples of the third-world, whose pagan gods demand infinitely more.

"If your God is the one true God," they want to know, "then why do you have it so easy?" They are right. And if all of this light religion seems funny to the heathens, it is even funnier in hell where, according to C.S. Lewis, "a moderated religion is as good for [the Devil] as no religion at all—and even more amusing."

I have begun to wonder whether or not our spiritual ancestors would even recognize us as the children of their faith. Or whether they, like the very demons we despise, would meet us and wonder, "Jesus I know and Paul I know about, but who are you?" (Acts 19:15). It would not be the first time.

Thirty years ago, Leonard Ravenhill wondered, "Has the blessed Spirit toned down His operations? . . . Did God close down His production lines after the Spirit had come upon Wesley, upon Finney, and such men? Were those leaders spiritual freaks? Were they oddities of grace, eccentrics who were a little 'off' in their spiritual operations?"[1]

Absolutely not! These are not some curious hybrids whose power and zeal are reproducible only under certain conditions. These are ordinary men and women like us, with one distinction: *they understood the full implications and logical consequences of what it means to "believe."*

There are two extremes tempting us in every generation, and this is the more recent one. Call it *secularism*: the tendency to be both *in* the world and *of* the world. Some of the liberal theologies of the past, and the contemporary worship of some churches today (though you can get none of them to admit it) have erred toward this extreme.

The other extreme is just as bad. *Monasticism* is the belief that the church should be neither *in* the world nor *of* the world. During the middle ages, thousands of monks believed this and sealed themselves off from the rest of society in order to focus on holy living. Some of them did quite well, but then, how much trouble can one find in a monastery?

Nevertheless, many of the "spiritual disciplines" of these men ranged from the very mundane to the bizarre. One fellow named St. Simeon buried himself up to his neck for several months, and later scaled a 60-foot pillar near Antioch, and sat on top of it for thirty years.

One monk named Ammoun lived the life of a hermit and, because he considered it vanity to care for himself, refused to bathe or even undress for several years.

Another one wandered naked around Mt. Sinai for fifty years.

One whole sect of them, known as the Bosci, lived in the open fields and grazed like cattle.

Arsenius, a monk of the fifth century, took the vow of complete poverty, but made it a point to walk through the marketplace once a year "because his heart rejoiced at the sight of all the things he didn't need."

Whole communities quarantined themselves from the very culture they were supposed to evangelize. And in this way, like Arsenius, they mocked the world from a distance. They did not convert it, nor even confront it.

Legalism, with its "touch not, taste not, handle not" morality, is a form of monasticism. It seeks to make men holy by denying them the pleasures of an ordinary, modern life.

No television.
No card games.
No "jungle music."
No mixed swimming.
No exceptions.

These were the rules of holiness churches fifty years ago, whose Church Disciplines read like an "us against the world" set of monastic vows.

Both of these extremes are counterfeit versions of true holiness. And just as counterfeits imply there is a real one somewhere else, there really is such a thing as authentic holy living. But what, exactly, is it? What does it look like? And who is it for?

The Meaning of Holy

When the Bible speaks of something as "holy," it is meant to be separate and uncommon. It is used to describe places, days, clothing, furniture, dishes, ground, water, oil, cities, words and people.

To be holy is to be *unique*. It is to be different than the rest.

Distinctively better. Reserved for special purposes.

But it also has a moral overtone. It describes those things which are set apart and totally consecrated for spiritual purposes. They are pure . . . sacred . . . dedicated to a single idea: that of pleasing and serving God and God alone.

When it is used of places, it would describe more a sanctuary than an all-purpose room. One of the tragedies facing the modern church is its utilitarian and pragmatic belief that sacred space can "double" as a gymnasium or banquet room, which is a peculiar attitude to hold, in view of the last 2,000 years of Christian worship.[2] Quite simply, you do not encounter God the way you dribble a basketball or pass the potatoes.

When the word "holy" is used to describe certain days, it means that Good Friday or Pentecost Sunday are unique in ways that the Fourth of July is not; even though the latter gets more attention.

It implies there is a reverence found in some attire that is absent in others, at least for those leading the worship.

Now when the word is used to describe people, they are said to be separate from the rest of their culture on account of their uncommon love for God and for others. Their white-hot passion to imitate Christ consumes them. Their radical, almost fanatical obsession with God and compulsion to think of nothing else—their familiarity and love for Him as though He were a good friend; and their conscientious conviction that everything they do and think is always under His gaze—sets them apart from the world . . . and the rest of so-called Christianity.

In one sense, they are closer to their pagan counterpart than to their church-going friends who are "nominally" Christian, because—like the pagan—they are an exaggerated version of their beliefs, whatever they are. They are hot, not cold. And to them, the most absurd position to take is the lukewarm position of middle ground. This explains, perhaps, why Jesus had an easier time with prostitutes and tax collectors than with the religious conservatives of His day.

But this is as far as it goes. Aside from the fact that, like the pagan, the holy man has thrown himself recklessly into his faith, he is nothing at all like the world in which he lives. He has a pure heart, a renewed mind, a sincere faith, and a holy passion for God. The Bible has said, and the happy experience of holy men in the past confirms, that whatever else holiness is, it is haveable for the ordinary people of our day. It is possible for common people to have an uncommon love for God. It is possible to do what is right and like it. It is possible to hear sermons on sin and *not* leave feeling guilty about them. It is possible to be the kind of person we admire. It is possible to really *know* we are pleasing God.

This is the sanctified life. This is the meaning of holiness. And this is the goal of all decent faith.

Holiness is a Pure Heart

When the Bible speaks of the heart it refers to the seat of all affections and desires. It is the epicenter of who we really are, buried deep beneath the layers of image, personality, attitude and behavior. This is the castle in which fear and faith; lust and love reside. It is the throne of hatred and forgiveness, worry and rest. The bottom line of our character. Everything we do, every pleasure we enjoy, every decision we make, every habit we form, all we desire and imagine, and who we are when no one's looking—all of these have a common denominator. And whatever it is, is the condition of our heart.

Now, just as we judge a car by "what's under the hood," we can judge a man by "what's in the heart." And, as Jesus said, we can know this by watching his actions. For it is not possible to act, think, speak, laugh, or cry for very long in a manner inconsistent with our heart. We may act better or worse than we really are for a moment or two, but as Vance Havner put it, "Whatever's in the well, will eventually come up in the bucket."

The condition of the heart determines the motive behind our actions. Whether an act is good or evil is more often determined by the motive of the heart than by the act itself.

There's a very old joke about a man who stood before God and insisted, "I'm ready for heaven."

"What makes you think so?" said the voice from the throne.

"Well, I gave to the poor, I went to church, I never cheated on my wife, I didn't drink, and I prayed twice a day."

"What you mean," said the Lord, "is that you took a tax deduction, you wanted people to think highly of you, you were afraid you'd get caught, you were allergic to alcohol, and you said grace before meals."

"I'm sorry," said the man, "I didn't think you'd know the difference."

Well, He does. And motive is everything. Even good deeds that are done from a selfish motive are evil in disguise. And bad things done from a pure motive are not as evil as we thought.

The Bible says our hearts may be purified from every selfish desire, and liberated to love God with all of our soul, mind and strength; and then to love our neighbor as much as we love ourselves (Mark 12:30-31). This, and nothing less, is entire sanctification. So purity in heart is the heart of the matter.

We may make mistakes because we are either ignorant or moody. We may holler at the kids or say more than we mean. We may rub people the wrong way. We may be, in our worst moments, irritable, overzealous, or downright obnoxious. But we care. We do not deny it.

And we don't excuse it as "just within my character" if we know it isn't in God's. And we do not ask each time that these transgressions be forgiven, but cleansed.

And while we may commit the same blunders as other people, there is a decided lack of self-interest in all of our frailty. We do not promote, pamper, please, defend, nor worry ourselves with ourselves the way others do.

If we have a pure heart, *we will love God for His own sake, and not only for ourselves.* Bernard of Clairveaux told us there were four levels of love, and that the two lowest were to love either ourselves or God for our own sake.

"When we suffer some calamity, some storm in our lives, we turn to God and ask for his help," he wrote, "this is how we, who only love ourselves, first begin to love God . . . because we have learned that we can do all things through him, and without him we can do nothing."

In this sense, many never graduate from the basement. But if our hearts are pure, they are stripped of all personal agendas in matters of piety and faith. God may fix our marriages, or He may not. He may cure our diseases or let them run their course. He may comfort us in our misery or leave us to work things out alone. He may vindicate us from the rumors which plunder our good name, or we may die as victims. But a pure heart knows Him, trusts Him, desires Him, and welcomes Him . . . whether He brings the goods or simply comes by himself.

There is no selfish interest in the pure, unmixed heart. Like Jesus, we do not have a part of us that is spiritual and another that is "all business." We cannot "lay our sanctification aside for a moment," which is the usual apology of a man about to do his own thing. We are not more obligated to be benevolent people because we know on which side our bread is buttered. We do not make "I know what the Bible says, but . . ." kinds of excuses.

Instead, we see the interests of others as more important than our own (Philippians 2:3). We refuse to make ourselves look good, even if it isn't always at the expense of someone else. We make a conscious and deliberate attempt to mine the good out of people and to rescue them from their badness.

If we have a pure heart, we love our neighbors . . . even those who live next to us (James 2:8).

We are not prejudiced (James 2:1).

We tolerate those who are difficult (1 Peter 3:16).

We truly love our enemies (Matthew 5:44).

We pray for those who persecute us . . . and not only to "heap burning coals upon their heads."

We forgive those who hurt us by turning the responsibility for punishment over to God, and by refusing to talk about it with others.

In our anger, we do not seek to protect our own interests, but those of God and others. We are more angry that men sin than that they sin against us.

A few years ago, I stumbled across the purest definition yet of what it means to be "crucified with Christ." It is so cutting, so penetrating, so high and lofty, that I keep it close by to spur me on.

> When you are forgotten or neglected or purposely set at naught, and you sting and hurt with the insult or the oversight, but your heart is happy, being counted worthy to suffer for Christ—*that* is dying to self.

> When your good is evil spoken of, when your wishes are crossed, your advice disregarded, your opinions ridiculed, and you refuse to let anger rise in your heart, or even defend yourself, but take it all in patient, loving silence—*that* is dying to self.

> When you can stand face to face with folly, waste, extravagance, spiritual insensibility, and endure it as Jesus endured it—*that* is dying to self.

> When you never care to refer to yourself in conversation, or to record your own good works, or itch after commendation; when you can truly love to be unknown—*that* is dying to self.

> When you see your brother prosper and have his needs met while your own needs are far greater and in desperate circumstances—*that* is dying to self.

> When you can receive correction and reproof from one of less stature than yourself, and can humbly sit inwardly as well as outwardly, finding no rebellion or resentment rising up within your heart—*that* is dying to self.[3]

And this . . . and nothing less . . . is a pure heart.

"Blessed are the pure in heart," said Christ, for these are the very spectacles through which we see God.

Holiness is a Renewed Mind

If your mind were a movie, what would it be rated? Could they show it in church? Too often, the answer is "no," and we hide behind the explanation that we live in a sensual and violent culture which plasters its images all over our minds during the trip to work in the morning, and during the commercial breaks on television that night.

"What does God expect?" we argue. "The media and publishers of our day make it impossible. John Wesley never had television. Augustine never read magazines. Thomas à Kempis didn't face a gauntlet of billboards every morning on his way to the office. It's just impossible to keep a pure mind."

More difficult? Yes.

Impossible? No. For the Bible says that once our minds are renewed, as we will discuss in a later chapter, we have a good conscience (1 Timothy 1:5).

We think Christianly (Philippians 2:5).

We do not dwell on evil thoughts (Psalm 19:14). We do not imagine ourselves hitting the lotto, winning the argument, undressing another lover, or strangling the person who has just cut in front of us.

We take captive *every* thought—not just some of them—and make it obedient to the lordship of Christ (2 Corinthians 10:5).

We scan the memory banks until we find things that are true, honest, pure, lovely, and of good report, and then we dwell on these things (Philippians 4:8).

We not only act, but *re*-act like Christians (1 Peter 2:21-23) .

We are not motivated by guilt, regret or obligation (1 Corinthians 4:3-4).

We not only *read* the Word of God, we *love* it (Psalm 119:97). We marinate our minds in it (Colossians 3:16).

We reason as Christ would (1 Corinthians 2:16). We love what He loves and hate what He hates.

We value humility and service (Romans 12:3, 7).

We live the fruit of the Spirit (Galatians 5:22-25).

It is one thing, as any failing Christian will tell you, to admire the mind of Christ. It is something entirely different to *have* it. We may want it, teach it, explain it, interpret it, profess it—and never *have* it. But those who truly crave it will one day find a growing semblance to the likeness of Christ.

Holiness is a Sincere Faith

The Bible calls this a "faith unfeigned," which means it is without hypocrisy (1 Timothy 1:5 KJV). That is, we do not say we believe something, then practice something else. One pastor admitted of his church, "We believe these things, we even teach these things, but we don't *do* these things."

But again, turning to the Scriptures, we find there is another kind of faith possible. When our hearts are pure and our minds renewed, it is possible to have a faith that makes the supernatural world seem like it is right next door. We can believe so strongly in God and the next world that we are not overwhelmed by this one.

Like Christ, we can kneel in our agony and pray, "not my will, but yours be done" (Luke 22:42). We may be asked by God to do unusual things—as was Noah, or to go out on a limb—as did Abraham, or to pray for miracles—as did Elijah, or even to look into the flames and sing hymns—as thousands of our ancestors have done.

We can come down to our last breath, knowing we simply must be right, and have the complete assurance, as Wesley did, that "God is with us." And we can do this because of an unshakable faith that has been hardened over the years. This kind is a breed apart from the rest of religion—modern Christianity included.

A holy faith will make us better than our reputations. It will go beyond the Ten Commandments, into the Sermon on the Mount. It will allow us, not only to abstain from grumbling, but to literally "rejoice and be glad" when we are persecuted for righteousness' sake (Matthew 5:10-12). It will not only keep us out of another person's sex life, but cause us *not* to imagine it in the first place (Matthew 5:28).

In these days of easy divorce and serial monogamies, we will honor our marriages because we wholly fear the God before whom we made our vows (Mark 10:8-9). Since our hearts have been purified from selfish interests, we do not ask about our "rights," nor worry ourselves with "having our own needs met." And when our spouses are selfish or insensitive, we do not hide behind the modern fig leaves of hurt and resentment, for true love "always protects, always trusts, always hopes, always perseveres" (1 Corinthians 13:7). Instead, we seek to nurture the marriage, not for a month or two, but for a lifetime if need be, because we believe, as Dietrich Bonhoeffer put it, that our "marriage is more than our love for each other . . . [it is] a link in the chain of generations, which God causes to come and to pass away to his glory . . . [it is] a post of responsibility towards the world and mankind." We will learn to love our partners as Christ loved the church—*that* much (Ephesians 5:25).

In the days of litigation our faith binds us to our word (Matthew 5:37). Our speech is pure and simple.

In the days of militant religion, we turn the other cheek and "resist not evil" (Matthew 5:39 KJV). We manifest holiness, not merely by boycotting the merchants or blocking an abortion clinic, but by our willingness to suffer whenever we are ridiculed or ignored. We speak kindly to those who oppose us because we are genuinely interested in *them*—not only their baby or their virtue. When we are offended, we do not take the law into our own hands, and we do not take a brother to

73

court (Matthew 5:25). We can be taken advantage of, and often are, but we entrust ourselves to Him who judges justly, for vengeance is His alone (1 Peter 2:23).

In the days of "show and tell" morality and the politics of virtue, our firm conviction that God sees *everything* not only keeps us away from evil, but in the good, even when no one else is looking and whether or not they care. We do our alms or slay our dragons in quiet, unseen places, not because it is politically correct, but because God "who sees what is done in secret, will reward us openly"—for better or worse—and we know it (Matthew 6:4).

In the days of family budgets and elaborate plans for retirement, our love for others causes us to live simply. We hold onto things loosely. We may or may not have money, but it is inconsequential to us since we have learned to store our treasures elsewhere (Matthew 6:20-21). We earn, we invest, we budget—but we do this to give our wealth away. We are happy with our income (Ecclesiastes 5:10). We tithe . . . at least (Matthew 23:23). We give to those who cannot repay us (Luke 6:35). And we don't talk about it (Matthew 6:3). We are not preoccupied with remodeling the summer cottage, or lollygagging around on exotic vacations, or finding the right satellite dish, or squeezing another buck out of the stock exchange, or anything else that will be meaningless the day after we are dead.

But in spite of the fact that the Bible portrays *this* as the normal Christian life, we have come to accept a faith that is considerably less dramatic. If you believe the polls, most of us pray less than five minutes, and read our Bibles for only nine minutes a day. We tithe less than two percent of our income. More than half seldom to never discuss religious matters at home. Only one in ten share their faith during the week. Nearly half of us fail in the simplest matters of integrity by padding our expenses or failing to report *all* our income. And far from being resilient, we are often only one crisis away from defecting the faith.

A growing number of people in our congregations are lured out of their marriages and into other affairs, emotional or otherwise, and many others endure bad marriages for the sake of their reputations alone. The more courageous file for divorce. At least one church in Texas has already instituted "divorce vows" because "sometimes even the most earnest vows cannot be kept." And so the pastor declares before the altar "that you are, before God, released from your bonds of marriage and are no longer husband and wife. You are free to face new futures as separate persons. Carry no burden of guilt or recrimination for what is past."[4]

And far from "settling matters quickly," in one metropolitan area, there were over 8,000 cases of litigation in one year involving persons on both sides of legal disputes who considered themselves "Christian."

It was estimated the legal fees of these cases alone exceeded $12 million.

While Americans still spend $40 billion on leisure, and another $32 billion to diet every year, they offer only $2 billion annually to missions, and spread it over 600 missionary-sending agencies. Even among church members, giving has dropped one and a half percent in the past 20 years because, according to one study, "members have formed attitudes toward money that are unconnected to their church or faith."[5] This is a depressing diagnosis when we consider Jesus said more about money than He did heaven or happiness.

The pastor was right, "we believe these things, we even teach these things, but we don't *do* these things." Even "holiness people," somewhat consoled by the apparent godlessness in the church, have taken refuge in the fact that, whatever else they may be, they are not as bad as the others. To them, holiness is a notch or two above the status quo. It does not occur to them that they themselves may barely be Christian, and their contemporaries not at all.

Holiness is a Passion for God

In the days of false prophets and a reckless fascination with the supernatural, holy people know their God. We may or may not be formally educated, but our fire comes from having been with Jesus. We may or may not prophesy or cast out demons, but there is a certain confidence in our stride, an authority in our voice, a familiarity in our prayers which says we are on a first-name basis with the One about whom others can only preach. Our intensity is magnetic, yet unnerving. Even our fun seems to flow naturally in the wake of this one holy passion.

Unlike the monk, we are not removed from the world. We are out in front of it. We deny ourselves pleasures the rest of the church enjoys. We keep disciplines the lukewarm church considers extreme. We not only *obey* the Word of God, we *love* it. We are not only *interested* in God, we *thirst* for Him. And these are the very things that push us to the edge of the rest of so-called "safe" Christianity; all to the applause of the church in heaven and to the utter embarrassment of the church on earth.

Four Assumptions

By now we have seen the height to which we are called when we are first converted, and though it may seem impossible and far out of reach, we can be sure of this: "God did not call us to be impure, but to live a holy life" (1 Thessalonians 4:7). From this we can make four assumptions, each critical to the biblical understanding of holiness.

First, ***this life is really possible.*** It's an invitation to the many, not an advertisement for the few. God's desire that His people be holy is as old as the nation of Israel (Exodus 19:6), and even precedes the giving of the Ten Commandments. A dozen times before the Law is finished, we are commanded to be a holy people because we serve a holy God. Twice in Deuteronomy, we are told to "circumcise our hearts," which involves a cutting away of things that are otherwise private and very sensitive; things which make us too much like everyone else. Ezekiel prophesied of "a new heart and a new spirit" (Ezekial 18:31) and Jesus spoke of those who were "pure in heart" (Matthew 5:8). David begged for "truth in the inner parts," and a pure heart, which is about the same thing (Psalm 51:6, 10). Paul said we were "created to be like God in true righteousness and holiness" (Ephesians 4:24), and Peter urged us to "be holy in all [we] do" (1 Peter 1:15). The writer of Hebrews encouraged us to "go on to maturity" (6:1) and to "pursue holiness, without which no one will see the Lord" (12:14).

Tragically, we have believed for too long that these references to holiness are relative with no definite end in sight. It is as though we may only get warmer, but never quite boil. The reformed theologian, Anthony Hoekema, argues this view by saying that Christ's ideal to "be perfect, as your heavenly Father is perfect . . . does not imply that we can attain this ideal in this life." But if this is true, then how seriously should we take the rest of the Sermon on the Mount?

Four verses earlier (Matthew 5:44), we are told to love our enemies and pray for those who persecute us. Is *this* possible? Or must this wait for the resurrection as well—when all of it will seem very easy? And what of the Beatitudes? Is it really asking too much *not* to boast or hold grudges? Is it all that extraordinary for us to keep our wives, keep our word, and keep our cool? Was Jesus really telling His disciples that day to shoot for the moon and be happy with the streetlight? Are there then two brands of holiness—His and ours? We are to be holy *"as he is holy."* And we are disciplined by God "that we may share (receive, partake) in *his* holiness," and not a better version of our own (Hebrews 12:10). Has God ever commanded more than He promised? And what are we to make of these desires for holiness? Are they of God? Or are they only the wishful thinking of frustrated mortals?

Absolutely not! We may never be perfect in the absolute sense, but this is not what is meant by the Scriptures anyway. The term "perfect" only means "complete or mature" and is used to describe the passing from adolescence into adulthood. It does not imply we will reach a point where no more progress is necessary. The only place outside of heaven where this is true, is hell. Instead, it means we can be as assured of our

Christian perfection as we are of our manhood or womanhood. We may never reach a point where we are so mature that we need not grow any longer. But this does not necessarily contradict our maturity or adulthood up to this point. Or put another way, to say I am not the man I should be, is not to say that I am not a man at all. And further, it is not to say I always was the man I am today. To the contrary, there are usually seasons in his life when the boy *becomes* the man. It is not something he merely improves or acknowledges. It is a rite of passage for him, complete with the responsibility, authority, and promise of a full-fledged adult. And once becoming a man, he will never be *more*, only better. So it is that Paul could insist that some of his followers were already perfect (or "mature," same Greek word), and pray that others soon would be (Ephesians 4:13; 2 Corinthians 13:9). To the good apostle, there was a time when they became what they were predestined to be: made after the likeness of Christ. From this point, their love for God and others would not be developed, but perfected. To say they needed to be more did not negate the idea that they were already something of what they needed to be, and that it was not just something *more*, but something quite *different* than their previous state.

So while we can never be absolutely perfect in this world, while we will always be confined by human limitations, it really is possible to live a life of holiness, to know that we are pleasing God, and to read the Bible without being embarrassed by passages others explain away. We can know that God answers prayer—even our prayers—and we can recover the love for God and purity of heart enjoyed by Adam and Eve in the garden.

If we ever believe that true holiness is less than this, we will become only comfortable with our Christian life, and soon after disillusioned by it.

Our second assumption is this: *even though this life is possible, it means a good deal more than we think it does.* Twenty years ago, D. Martyn Lloyd-Jones warned us against "reducing the teaching of Scripture down to our level of obedience." This is the danger of "defining deviancy down," which we discussed in chapter three. By this, we decide that since there is so much sin in this world, maybe we can learn to live with it; and since biblical holiness is so hard to come by, maybe we can learn to live without it.

"We are so spiritually *sub*normal," wrote Leonard Ravenhill, "that to be just normal seems to make us *ab*normal."

And the cure for this is never to simply "consecrate" ourselves and live with our inconsistencies. We are not holy because we say we are. We are holy because we have learned to say "no" to ungodliness, and we have renewed our minds until our desires are those of Christ, himself, and our hearts have been purified from selfishness. And, as we will learn in the following chapter, this cannot happen in a pre-determined instant, whenever we want it to. We must be drawn by love, fueled by desire, disciplined by God and prompted by the Spirit.

This is our third assumption: *even though this life is possible, it means a good deal more than we think it does, and because of this, **most who profess to be entirely sanctified . . . aren't.*** And this is our real nemesis.

There are thousands of "entirely sanctified" people who think they are such, not because their hearts are pure or their minds renewed, but because they once prayed to have it this way, then left believing it happened that instant. Then, just like they were told, they professed it before others who had the same experience themselves. And they have been glibly professing it all along. It does not bother some that they love themselves and defend themselves the way unholy people do. To themselves, they are still sanctified because they have jumped through the hoops of certain prayers and testimonies, without ever stopping to ask themselves whether or not they resemble the lives of David, Paul or Christ.

And the real tragedy, of course, is that they end up settling for less. They are very much like the people of Jerusalem: busy milling about in the Temple, safe in their staid religion, now thousands of years old, while the very best God has to offer is left outside the city, on a hill overlooking the whole mess . . . waiting . . . and weeping . . . over what might have been.

Having said this, we must return to our first and final assumption: *even though this life is possible, it means a good deal more than we think it does, and because of this, most who profess to be entirely sanctified— aren't, **nevertheless this life is STILL possible,*** or whole sections of the New Testament go unexplained. Let's not become so discouraged by the blurred copy we see in others or even within ourselves, that we despise even the original. For hidden inside our deep desires for a better life is the fundamental hope that such a life is somehow possible. And if we lose it, we have lost the essence of our faith.

Let us not become so disheartened by the abundance of fool's gold, that we forget a vein of the real gold always lies somewhere nearby. To have it, we need only admit that what we now have is not enough, and then we must set out to find it. And once we do, we will know the paradox of a hungering soul satisfied at last . . . only to hunger on.

NOTES:
[1] Leonard Ravenhill, *Revival Praying*, (Minneapolis: Bethany House, 1962), p. 57.
[2] There are, of course, exceptions down through history where the people of God were compelled by poverty or persecution to meet in the homes of members.

Nevertheless, the creation of some sort of "sacred space" has been as central to the idea of Christian Worship as liturgy or holy days. See Robert Webber, *Worship is a Verb*, (Nashville: Abbott-Martyn, 1992), pp. 196-198. See also J.F. White, *Introduction to Xn Worship*, (Nashville: Abingdon, 1990), pp. 88-121.

[3] Cited by John MacArthur in *The MacArthur New Testament Commentary: Ephesians*, (Chicago: Moody, 1986), p. 299.

[4] "Ceremony Eases Pain of Divorce," Associated Press (September 16, 1980), cited by Richard Fowler in *Winning By Losing*, (Chicago: Moody, 1986), pp. 54–55.

[5] The study was done by Empty Tomb, Incorporated for the years 1968–1992, and funded by a Lilly Endowment. Reported in *National & International Religion Report*, (February 6, 1995): p. 4.

CHAPTER 7

ALMOST— BUT NOT YET

The Frustration and Hope of Progressive Sanctification

In Greek mythology, the greedy king, Sisyphus, was condemned by the gods to roll a huge stone up a treacherous slope, only to watch it tumble back to the bottom, where he would begin his sentence all over again.

That pretty well summarizes the frustration many of us feel in our spiritual walk. The Christian life is just one hill after another. Take, for instance, the biker peddling furiously to reach the top of a high slope, anticipating an effortless glide down the other side. But as he reaches the top, what does he see? Another hill! Even steeper than the one he has just conquered.

Now here is his dilemma: He truly wants to finish the journey. He has heard from others that the land over the top is worth the trek, and that once he is there he can rest. He believes this, but there—at the top of one hill, and still at the bottom of another—he begins to question his decision to go on.

"Why is this so difficult?" he wonders. "Maybe I'm not ready for this."

All his energy and fascination is gone . . . wasted on the first hill. He has nothing left. He considers turning around, but that would be to concede the land above him. And he would only want to try it again. So there he sits. Beat. Overwhelmed. Intimidated. But stuck with his decision to go on.

Sound familiar?

Hang on.

Within the Christian life, there are only three predicaments, with varying degrees in each. The first we'll call *"Dead in Christ."* These people are not dead in the literal sense, of course. Most are regular church attenders. Many tithe, teach, or sing in the choir. Some occupy high positions within the local church (or beyond). A few even bear the label of a "pillar" in the church. Most can tell you of a time when they "accepted Christ" by coming to the altar or reciting a prayer. But they have never grown since. Their testimonies are shallow and stale. They are orthodox in their beliefs, indeed they are very moral people who seldom do anything "wrong." Yet there is a conspicuous lack of seriousness to their religion. They are noticeably unenthusiastic, except about other things. There is neither fruit nor service to their lifestyle. They can see suffering and not feel obligated to relieve it. They can sit unmoved through stirring messages and solemn worship without ever taking their pulse. They are only momentarily affected by what Jonathan Edwards called, "'wouldings'—those weak inclinations that lack convictions, that raise us but a little above indifference."[1] They are "good pagans." But they are as sound asleep as any other.

And since Jesus promised to fill only those who continually "hunger and thirst for righteousness" (Matthew 5:6), these poor and malnourished souls haven't eaten in years. They differ from other heathens only in this: bad pagans are not hungry and never were; good pagans were hungry once—just before they got "saved"—and having since testified to their filling, have never hungered again. They ate once, and died shortly after with a full stomach.

The second predicament, we'll call *"Blessed Assurance."* These people are good, confident Christians who live obediently, worship enthusiastically, examine themselves regularly. They love from the gut. They do not claim to be perfect, but they're a great deal more than they were. Their security is based on their intimacy with God. They know that they are "accepted in the beloved" (Ephesians 1:6 KJV), and do not measure themselves against the rules of the church or the personalities on the platform.

The third predicament is the most popular, and lies somewhere between the Dead in Christ and the Blessed Assurance crowd. This is the category of the *"Almost—But Not Yet."* Like the weary biker, their hearts are set on good things, but their minds and judgments are still caught in the daily grind of what they now call the "real world." They are deeply sentimental towards God. They love to worship. They cry during the songs, and even discuss the sermon over dinner. They admire holy people. They love the environment of a good church, and crave the simplicity and innocence of a deep faith in God, and even leave church every Sunday determined to have it for themselves. But after a few days, their "ought-to" intention disintegrates into "should-have" guilt. Soon after, failure turns to frustration, and they become harder and harder on themselves.

"I have so far to go," one of them confesses at the altar, rehearsing everything she's done wrong that week. "Sometimes I think it's impossible."

"I wish I were as good as my reputation," says another man over lunch. "I am trying so hard, but I really don't think what I'm doing is all that bad."

An older woman closes her Bible following a study of the Sermon on the Mount. "Oh well," she blurts out, "nobody's perfect, but we're all trying."

All of them are saying the same thing. Some are very outspoken about their struggles, even testifying to them in public. Others are more private, afraid to come out from behind their nice reputations and admit to their frustration and brokenness. For some, the hurt crystallizes into cynicism, until they deny even the possibility of holy living, and seem to delight in bursting the bubble of anyone who claims it for himself. One such person asked John Wesley if he knew anyone who was entirely sanctified.

"If I knew one, I would not tell you," said Wesley, "for you are like Herod: you only seek the child to slay it."

Now, what happens when people in each of these three predicaments confront a good message on holiness, or wade through the last chapter of this book? For those dead in Christ, it is pure affirmation and no challenge. They read the Sermon on the Mount as though it were their autobiography. And so, to paraphrase Socrates, "they know not, and know not that they know not."

The Blessed Assurance crowd are encouraged that the subject of holiness was given a hearing, and are inspired with a mature hope and a resolve to go even further in their Christian walk.

Like the weary biker, the "Almost—But Not Yet" people stand on top of things just conquered, and gaze up at the life just described and secretly wonder whether or not they have the backbone for it. Some quit and go to the bottom. Others plod on. But most just sit in the middle, willing to live the holy life should it ever come easy, but too intimidated to go after it.

We pray for the first group. We celebrate the second. But we grow with the third.

Growing Pains

Stand back and look at the categories again, and a few observations will surface. The most obvious is that *conversion is a passage from the first category, right into the second.* The new convert only rarely gets caught in the Almost—But Not Yet. Instead, he suddenly feels alive. Nearly every verse he reads is like a well-aimed missile, telegraphed by God for his personal experience. He snatches up a copy of the New Testament and underlines every third verse. His religion still has the element of surprise. His testimonies are fresh. His joy is intoxicating, which explains why so many established Christians want to disciple him. Peculiarly, those who seem most interested in discipling these people are, themselves, often stuck in the Almost—but Not Yet predicament. And it is not the thought of passing something on but the hope of catching something in return that entices them.

Unfortunately, the sun sets early in the land of Blessed Assurance, as the realities of a carnal nature cloud the horizon. Like the rich young ruler, we find our confidence over having kept all the commandments, darkened by Christ's insistence that we still lack one thing to be perfect (see Matthew 19:21). Free salvation suddenly seems expensive. What once was easy, gets hard. The rest we were promised becomes the rest we must find. First we loved flowers, now we must learn to hate weeds. That means hard work and discipline.

This should not discourage us. *It is very normal to move from one predicament to another.* In fact, the healthy Christian life is really a mixture of Blessed Assurance and the Almost—but Not Yet. Indeed, those who live exclusively in the land of **Blessed Assurance** are probably **Dead in Christ.** For the only difference between the callused and the confident Christian is whether or not he has earned his rest after trudging up the slopes of Almost—But Not Yet.

One final observation, and this is the most encouraging: *all growth occurs on the incline.* Draw near to the holy men and women of the past, and you will sense the doubt in their blessed assurance. It is not a fear of losing their souls, but an obsession with the holiness of God that drove them to extremes. This is only natural, for the better one sees an original, the more critical his eye towards a mere copy.

Thomas à Kempis, a German monk of the 15th century, carefully examined everything about himself, and, at times, concluded that he was "more ready for perdition than for life."

John of the Cross, a 16th century Carmelite monk, said there were three stages of Christian growth (beginners, progressives, and the perfect), and considered himself a beginner.

John Wesley wrote a tract called *The Character of a Methodist*, to define what he meant by Christian perfection, but prefaced the whole work with a disclaimer: "not as though I had already attained."

. . . which sounds a lot like the words of another follower of Christ (Saint Paul), whose writings are said to be not only honest, but inspired.

So let's not become overwhelmed by our restlessness. The path from sin to holiness is not a momentary decision, but a journey involving many exciting, and sometimes agonizing discoveries.

It is a passing from unconscious depravity to conscious depravity, commenced by learning that we know not.

We may feel overwhelmed at times, and discouraged by our apparent lack of progress. There may be seasons when we feel stuck in the quagmire of habits. But if we will stop for a moment and look around, we will see that this, too, is a well-traveled path towards the image of Christ. There is, in fact, a fairly common pattern of growth from sin to sanctification, with various stages along the way. This is called "progressive sanctification." And for the purpose of marking the progress of those living on the incline, a typical pattern looks like this:

Stage One: New Life!

As we've said earlier, the typical conversion experience is a radical jump from the "dead in Christ" to "blessed assurance." Immediately following our conversion, there is a general feeling of relief. We know our sins have been forgiven, and feel we have a personal relationship with God. Sometimes, this is a very emotional experience. Other times, it is not. Like the woman anointing the feet of Jesus (Luke 7:47), it depends largely on how much has been forgiven. From this genuine conversion, there emerges a new person whose opinions about sin, self, and God have all been changed. We are learning that God genuinely loves us, and as a result, we have a new desire to please God and a new sensitivity to anything that might hinder that relationship. These two components, a new desire and a new sensitivity, will play a significant role in our growth in holiness.

Along with this, there is a sudden increase in our knowledge of the Bible as we soak up everything in front of us. We learn what we love. We develop a natural affinity for the people of God, and listen to their advice and experiences. We feel like novices, like adults who have finally gotten serious about life and gone back to school. We feel so "behind" in our understanding of the Bible, and work tirelessly to recover the lost years.

Stage Two: Settling In!

In this stage, we continue to discover the truth about ourselves, and in response, surrender ourselves to God. One by one, we are called to break old habits or start new ones, and we may struggle with how to do it, but the decision to do it at all has already been made.

The danger in this stage is that, as our fascination with Christ grows dimmer, we turn to other sources besides the Scriptures and our converted consciences to determine for ourselves what is the will of God. We buy best-selling books and God-on-the-fly study Bibles. We turn to talk-show study groups, or the noise of Christian radio. We ask questions of others we ought first to be asking Christ in prayer.

The trouble with this is that no one else can operate the way the Holy Spirit can. And churches or prophets who try to, usually kill the patient. Either we find ourselves out of step with God's true will, confronting some hidden sins and leaving others alone, or we merely conform to a set of convictions we really don't believe.

Given His own time, the Spirit will gradually reveal to us the connection between our actions and our will.

By peeling back our lust, we see our wantonness.

By opening a private discussion over our anger and cynicism, the Holy Spirit leads us to see that our real sin is pride.

With time, God's searchlight penetrates the fog of our fear or skepticism and shows us our raw unbelief at the bottom.

Like an experienced guide, He leads us through the caverns of hurt feelings and unforgiveness, to find ourselves deep in the center, worshiping at our own shrine.

He shows us the vengeance we have hidden inside our justice, the self inside our ambition, the rebellion inside our courage, the arrogance inside our kindness, the lust inside our love, the condescension inside our mercy, the prejudice inside our wisdom, the cruelty inside our discipline.

These things take time. They do not come as a random flash of insight at the moment of conversion. They are the rare discoveries of men and women who have been often alone with themselves and God.

Stage Three: A Growing Restlessness!

Now firmly on the incline, we feel a growing restlessness with a desire for God to finish His work in us. The discoveries of the previous stage have left their mark, making us feel worse about ourselves and not better. But this, too, is only normal. After all, the stronger the love for God, the more intense is the hatred for anything that offends Him. Like most people in the Almost—But Not Yet predicament, we are sure of our salvation, but we become increasingly frustrated with ourselves and our shortcomings. We know we will never be *absolutely* perfect, but it has to get better than this.   And we are convinced, through the plain Scripture, that it *has* for some, and we want it for ourselves.

Whether it is the last gasp of a dying sinful nature, or the resurrected fear of what might happen once we are no longer living for ourselves, these are the final birth pangs which will send us into a whole new experience.

Stage Four: Complete Devotion to God and His Holiness

For some, this is another name for entire sanctification. But at this point, it is important to lay a couple of superstitions to rest. First, *it is less important what we call this, or even how it happens, than it is whether or not it has really happened at all.* I have witnessed whole arguments for sanctification built around terminology alone. I have seen committees go toe-to-toe over the "quantification of sin" or "the eradication of the sinful nature" until I was fairly certain that—whatever holiness may or may not be—there was precious little left among the gladiators in the room. Odd as it is, we lost holiness in an argument over sanctification.

Too many of us reduce the power of God to a single experience, then cannonize it and measure our brothers and sisters accordingly. And in this we desire orthodoxy more than love, and sanctification more than God, himself.

Second, contrary to much of what is heard, *the passing from restlessness (stage 3) to complete devotion (stage 4) may or may not happen in an instant.* That it must, is more the doctrine of John Wesley's followers than of Wesley, himself.

To Wesley, entire sanctification was the "total death to sin and an entire renewal in the image of God." Of course, this implied "a last moment wherein [sin] does exist, and a first moment wherein it does not." But for Wesley, this moment was more a logical conclusion than the prize or trophy of our faith. Most of Christianity was lived in the long seasons of what he called "gradual change." For some, this "last moment wherein sin does exist" was a subtle, almost imperceptible event compared to the celebrated gains made in the preceding months or years.

Further, Wesley argued (and Scripture seems to support it) that one could not advance in the journey toward sanctification without the Holy Spirit drawing him.

And once they were entirely sanctified, Wesley advised them "not to speak of it to them that know not God, nor to others, without some particular reason."

Yet even before he died, a colleague named John Fletcher (whose writings Wesley, himself, published) put a little different spin on Wesley's teaching of sanctification. Wesleyan scholar Donald Dayton has pointed out that, while Wesley used thirty proof texts from which he preached the doctrine of entire sanctification, his preaching was conspicuously void of the book of Acts. None of the thirty texts were founded there. Fletcher's preaching had a different emphasis. According to Dayton, "the book of Acts is cited more than any other biblical source in his collected *Works*."[2] Thus, he began to use terminology like "second blessing" or "baptism of the Spirit" or "modern Pentecost" to summarize the experience of entire sanctification, terms which are rarely seen in Wesley's writings.[3]

This kind of pressing for the moment of entire sanctification prevailed in much of holiness doctrine throughout the second great awakening (1800–1835), and was finally crystallized into a doctrine by a woman with a strong dislike for formal theology.

Phoebe Palmer was a doctor's wife, whose own experience in 1837 became the catalyst for her teaching on entire sanctification. She insisted in an almost magical power of the altar experience. Her view that the "altar sanctifieth the gift" (an idea she borrowed from Matthew 23:19) meant that the crisis of entire sanctification was the consequence for anyone who totally consecrated himself to God. The hard questions came later. Like Wesley advised (and she knew his writings better than any of us), she "strongly insisted on the instantaneous," but not to "advance the gradual change in believers," as Wesley said. For her, the moment of consecration around an altar was the prize awaiting every evangelist who preached the higher life.

The "shorter way" she called it. And by this she meant the path to holiness did not need to be as long and excruciating as Wesley first suggested. It could be "had" anytime. And what was more, if it was not, the seeker committed the unpardonable sin of refusing a gift from God, for which the punishment was hell. There you have it: holiness or hell. Any questions?[4]

The most notable distinction between Wesley's teaching and that of Phoebe Palmer was the camp meeting. At the beginning of the 19th century, Christians began a lengthy fascination with the outdoor camp meeting, in which the long and arduous journey towards Christian perfection was compressed into a few short days in the open air, initiated with a trip to the altar and confirmed with the first testimony.

It was a re-packaged Wesley, tailor made for the frontier revival.

Even so, today much of what is taught on holiness more closely resembles the doctrine of Palmer than Wesley, who has at least one denomination named after him.

The typical sermon one is likely to hear on holiness sounds like this:

1. Recognize that God wants you to be holy,
    and believe that you can be if you are
    willing.

This appeal is usually made with references to God's holiness, and a stiff warning that we better be holy too, if we have any plans for heaven. After all, holiness is a command. And those who are not holy, disobey the command. Disobedience is sin. And you know where sinners go.

2. Commit every area of your life to the
    will of God, especially "that one
    sin" you keep holding back.

Unfortunately, every generation has had their own idea of what "that one sin" was likely to be. In the early camp meetings, high-winded preachers railed against the evils of horse racing and whiskey. Sixty years ago, it was "theatrical diversions" and "the reading of humorous and comical books." A friend of mine remembers when she couldn't read the funnies on Sunday. Seventy years ago it was "frivolous conversation" and "baseball games."[5] Today, the hot buttons are lust and unforgiveness. To be sure, each of these needs a hearing, but the mere absence of them in one's life does not make him a model citizen in heaven anymore than "paying taxes" makes him a model citizen on earth.

3. Ask God to fill you with His Holy Spirit,
    and believe that He has. Now begin
    to live the holy life.

If this sounds a little like "name it—claim it," you're getting the idea. This is holiness at the drive-through window. In this line of thinking, the prayer becomes the center of the whole experience. The agonies of self-examination and self-denial—so typical of early Christians—are suddenly compressed into a few minutes around the altar. The "old man," as the Bible calls our sinful nature, is not gradually put down, he is shot and buried in the same day.

4. Confirm that God has sanctified you by
   testifying to your experience.

Some have warned that if we do not testify, the sanctification will never last.

Though Palmer never intended it, many of those professing the higher life were only different from the others in their testimony and not in their life. They followed the shorter way right down to the altar and, thereafter, never looked back. As we will see in the following chapter, they never defeated sin, they only ignored it. Any sin or shortcoming which followed their "second blessing" was simply annexed into their definition of "holy but human." That is, the ditches were moved and the road widened to allow for things not altogether holy, but, nevertheless, a scar on the hide of those who just got blessed. In truth, men and women have been made holy through both kinds of experiences. Wesley and Palmer have each had their day. But those who side exclusively with Palmer, and we have already hinted at this, need to consider the apparent lack of Bible passages commanding an instantaneous cleansing whenever you are ready and willing. To be sure, dozens refer to the life itself, but very few pertain to the moment of entry.[6]

The Scripture seems to focus more on the miracle than the doctrine. For the doctrine itself is as much intertwined with our experience as with the Bible. Indeed, the "second blessing" paradigm seems peculiarly confined to a single period in history, and even then, only within those denominations which espoused the camp meeting.

For me, the stage of complete devotion to God is like the gradual healing of a patient who is very sick with an infection in his arm. He has treated it himself, but with no success, and so he finally consents to see his doctor, who promptly sends him to the hospital for an intravenous dose of high-octane antibiotics. Two days later, he returns home with a bottle of horse pills and a list of instructions to soak the wound. Within a few weeks, the infection has healed completely, and the patient has full use of his arm. He is back in good health, and growing stronger, but he cannot always tell you the *day* he got better.

It was first a process, and later a crisis (perhaps the fever broke or the blockage opened up), and finally a process again. He knows the trip to the doctor probably saved his arm, but that it wasn't healed the day he left the hospital. He knows he is now fully recovered and probably was long before he ran out of horse pills. But he still can't nail down the exact time.[7]

For some, this stage of complete devotion to Christ comes only after a giant fire is set inside them. For others, it will be the warming of a heart gradually set ablaze. But in every case, we can know what it is, we can know it is possible, we can know we're progressing, and we can know when we are finally healed.[8]

Stage Five: We Earnestly Desire What We Already Possess

To carry the analogy a bit further, the recovering patient must keep two things in mind. The first is that he will never be so healthy that he cannot get sick again. The moment he becomes careless, he is leaving himself open for another bout with infection. The second is that, even though he is always vulnerable to infection, he need not succumb to it. And the surest prevention is to improve his stamina. After all, health and strength are close, but different conditions. Anyone who is not strong will not be healthy for long against the ever-dangerous invasion of those things which war against him. So it is that we are called to "perfect holiness out of reverence for God" (2 Corinthians 7:1), and to "live in order to please God . . . more and more" (1 Thessalonians 4:1).

In this sense, we are not absolutely perfect anymore than one can be absolutely full of either food or love. We may be very satisfied for the moment, but if we are normal, we will one day want more to eat and more to love. The fullness of God is exhaustible, always fluctuating, and does not describe the amount of piety in our lives, so much as the temperature of our devotion. Like any white-hot substance, it can always get hotter. And to those for whom it has, it is still not hot enough.

"To have found God and still to pursue Him is the soul's paradox of love," wrote A.W. Tozer, "scorned indeed by the too-easily-satisfied religionist, but justified in happy experience by the children of the burning heart."

Travel Tips for the Weary Traveler

As I have already stated, the journey towards holiness is exactly that—a journey. It is a gradual incline with no clear formulas, punctuated briefly with milestones, which serve to remind us that we really are making progress—in spite of how we feel.

And since there are no formulas, we'll not finish this chapter with the typical "how to be sanctified" recipe. Instead, I want to offer a couple of travel tips to the sanctified-in-process who, like the weary biker, find themselves somewhere between the bottom and the land over the top. Think of me, not as the final authority, but as one who has spent years on the incline, having experienced both the joy and the frustration of life between the almost—but not yet.

If you find yourself living somewhere on the incline—desiring the land over the top, yet fighting the pull from below—the first thing you can do is *admit your condition.* ⭐

There is a danger inside holiness churches where people "sanctify" one another through peer pressure and reform. Those who would be holy "fake it until they make it." The "powers that be" look down their noses at those who are not holy, and the poor people know it, and so one day after the sermon, they rally up the courage to come to an altar and "consecrate it." After a brief prayer, they are slapped on the back and told to "believe in their heart." But only days later, they find the magic prayer has not produced the kind of results they were promised. The woman senses anger smoldering inside when her husband does not pick up after himself. The teenage boy gives in again to peer pressure. The divorcee cannot keep her skin from crawling when *he* enters the room. And so on.

They believe that entirely sanctified people don't struggle with these kinds of things. And so they counterfeit the good life, pretending in public to have slain these dragons, yet they are devoured by them every day at home. They become frustrated with themselves, but keep these frustrations private for fear they will tip their hand, and someone—God forbid—may argue they were never sanctified and maybe not even saved.

After years of this charade, they learn to pay more attention to reputation than to reality. It becomes more important what others believe them to be, than who they really are.

"I am appalled to see how much of the change which I thought I had undergone lately was only imaginary," wrote C.S. Lewis to his friend, Malcolm Muggeridge. "It is to . . . dream that you have waked, washed, and dressed, and then to find yourself still in bed."

The end result of all this is that they are stuck with a "touch not, taste not, handle not" legalism which only handcuffs their sinful nature, but never destroys it.

For those who are caught in this predicament—who feel they are crippled and out of step with those saintly heroes of the past, and waiting in hope that one day the Christ will walk by—the journey to wholeness begins by admitting your condition to one or two other trusted friends who truly love you. Find someone who is not put off by your unholiness, ask them to pray faithfully for those seasons to come in your life, when God will grow the faith that He began. You may want to confide in a pastor, a Sunday school teacher, a counselor, a colleague or a good friend. Give them permission to ask you about your progress, from time to time.

Of course, this is not the prayer of someone seeking a license to do his own thing. It is the cry of a heart that has tried many, many times . . . and failed. It is the hope and desire of a weary traveler stuck on the incline.

Once we have rallied support for ourselves, we must *stay focused.* When Jesus was asked the most important command, He responded without hesitation.

"Love the Lord your God with all your heart, soul, mind and strength," He said, "and love your neighbor as yourself." And when the Pharisee agreed, Christ told him he was not far from the kingdom of God (see Mark 12:30-34). It was the only time in the Bible that Christ and the Pharisees agreed on anything, and it was the closest any Pharisee ever got to the Kingdom. So let's not fritter the hours away with second tier questions:

Are you reading your Bible enough?

Are you giving enough to missions?

Did you say too much over dinner the other night?

Who is the last person you led to Christ?

Do you watch R-rated movies?

Did you lose your temper at the softball game?

. . . and you call yourself a *Christian* ?!!

These are the little foxes that spoil the vine for us. Our minds get cluttered with these questions (important as they are) until we are only juggling holiness, at best, waiting nervously to "fumble" something. This only frustrates us, while we covet the spirituality of those who excel in the very areas which defeat us.

A famous preacher of an earlier day wrote a
book about his early search for a full life
in Christ. He told of his struggle for
holiness—hours of prayer for purification
from selfishness and wrong desires. He told
how he guarded his every word and action,
struggling to bring them into conformity with

God's will.

Finally exhausted by the pursuit, he con-
tracted TB and spent a year in a sanitarium.
There he met a young woman of his denomination
who was recuperating from the same disease.
She seemed so tranquil and pure. He watched
her for weeks and became convinced that she
had found the secret that eluded him. One
night as he struggled in prayer, he felt he
could wait no longer. He rose to find her,
determined to ask her for the way to peace.

Before he could leave, there was a knock
on his door. There she stood, her face
contorted as her body shook with sobs.

"Brother Harry," she gasped, "I've watched
you all these weeks. If anyone has found the
secret of holiness, it's you. I've *got to
know.*"[9]

If most of us were honest with ourselves, we would see that the greater part of our frustration has less to do with Christ and more to do with how we stack up against Mr. or Mrs. Got-It-All-Together. The irony, of course, is that we end up envying those who envy us. Much of our guilt comes, not from having disappointed God, but from having failed in the expectations of our good contemporaries, who may now think less of us. So we measure ourselves against ourselves, then re-align ourselves or compensate for our bad behavior, enough to get along with our circle of friends. All of this makes us very popular with each other, but strangely out of step with heaven, where the goal is progress, not reputation, where the standard is Christ and not others, and where the real competition is sin—the lowest common denominator.

The writer of Hebrews reminds us that Christ is not merely the author of our faith, but the "perfecter" of it as well (Hebrews 12:2). And that He, having already gone before us, is in the best position to move us up the incline and into the land over the top. And as we progress, we will find, as did "Christian" in *Pilgrims Progress* (by John Bunyan), that the sins which weigh us down grow lighter and lighter as we make the climb, until finally and all at once, the last of them has disappeared.

NOTES:
[1] Cited by Richard Foster and James B. Smith, *Devotional Classics: Jonathan Edwards*, (San Francisco: Harper, 1993), p. 19.
[2] Donald Dayton, *Theological Roots of Pentecostalism*, (Peabody:

Hendrickson, 1987), pp. 52–53.

[3] To be sure, John Wesley did use the term "second blessing." J.A. Wood notes four different occasions where Wesley used the term (See J.A. Wood, *Wesley on Perfection*, [Salem: H.E. Schmul], pp. 104–105). I am only suggesting that the term was less prominent to Wesley than to his successors, and that its popularity in the next generation of holiness preaching represented a significant shift in the doctrine and process of entire sanctification.

[4] There is some debate as to whether Phoebe Palmer was that different from Wesley in her teachings on holiness. Church historian Melvin Dieter has taken the side that Wesley's view of gradual sanctification is real, but overemphasized, as are his differences with Phoebe Palmer. While Dieter admits that Palmer was the mother of modern name-it-claim-it theology, he maintains that her comments are very compatible with mainstream Methodism of the early nineteenth century. The aberrations in the holiness doctrine, says Dieter, came from writers who were one generation removed from Palmer (early twentieth century). It is my view that, while Palmer's theology was never in stark contrast to Wesley's, she, nevertheless, emphasized certain views of his and thus pulled him out of context. For example: (1) She moved the work of entire sanctification closer to the beginning of one's Christian experience. While Wesley believed that it was available to everyone, and even that everyone should seek it from their early conversion, he placed a greater emphasis on the gradual growth and cleansing of the believer before his experience of entire sanctification. (2) She shifted the emphasis of sanctification from dying, to consecration. While Wesley likened the crisis of entire sanctification to the death of an already dying man, Palmer equated it to the decision of one's will to consecrate himself fully to God. This allowed for more dramatic and sensational experiences, and shifted the burden for total cleansing from God (who would do the cleansing) to the seeker (who would be cleansed). Wesley held the two in balance, believing that holiness was as much the result of waiting on God as it was commitment to the disciplines. (3) She went beyond the writings of Wesley which emphasized the urgency of Christian perfection to the harsh ultimatum of holiness or hell. In his "Plain Account," and both sermons on Christian perfection, Wesley's style was to reason with his detractors, rather than to serve up the blessing in "either/or" language. This approach was, of course, not peculiar to Mrs. Palmer. It was typical of her day. But it, nevertheless, opened the door for extremes and abuses a generation later. (4) She insisted on the public testimonies of those who professed to have the "second blessing," even warning that if they did not testify, they would lose the blessing. Wesley acknowledged that the desire to testify would be irresistible since "the fire would be so hot," but urged caution and humility, and never threatened the loss of the blessing, since entire sanctification was less a Pentecostal experience and more a state of the heart to him. Dieter is right in charging that Palmer is not solely responsible for the doctrines which followed her. These were the problems of those who out-Palmered Phoebe Palmer. But we have missed a significant turn in the road of holiness history if we minimize Palmer's theology and her vast influence on modern holiness thought. Historians are still divided over the interpretation of Palmer's writings (though not their impact). The reader is encouraged to weigh these arguments, along with those by Thomas Oden, Donald Dayton and Melvin Dieter, and decide the matter for himself.

[5] *Manual of the Pilgrim Holiness Church*, (Cincinnati: Pilgrim Holiness Advocate, 1926), Sec. 74, Paragraph 6; p. 38.

[6] The two most prominent passages for an instantaneous sanctification experience are said to be the Greek renderings of Romans 12:1 and 1 Thessalonians

5:23-24. Nevertheless, the doctrine of instantaneous sanctification is often implied through reason and logic, even when it is not clearly stated in the text. Within the proper parameters, this is safe and somewhat necessary, as other Christian doctrines (i.e., the Trinity, instantaneous salvation) are derived in much the same manner.

[7] The past few generations of holiness taught us that entire sanctification was usually instantaneous (entered through an act of consecration), but allowed for a gradual process for some. What I have done here is invert that tradition by emphasizing the gradual cleansing as the norm, while still allowing for an instantaneous sanctification experience. It seems important, at this juncture in history, to once again clearly separate the acts of conversion and entire sanctification by putting more time between them, and calling for a thorough examination of our mind, motives and nature, in order to know what, exactly, was sanctified. This seems consistent with Wesley's sermons on *Christian Perfection* (there were two), and with his *Plain Account of Christian Perfection* (1766), as well as his reflections a year later when he wrote, "I believe in a gradual work both preceding and following that instant . . . I believe it is usually many years after justification; but that it may be within five years or five months after it. I know of no conclusive argument to the contrary," John Wesley, *The Works of John Wesley*, third edition, Volumn 11, (Grand Rapids: Baker reprint, 1979), p. 446. Whatever the era, and however convincing the arguments for an instantaneous or gradual experience, we may lay it down as a fundamental principle that we are to be more concerned with the what and why of sanctification (What did it resolve? Why is it necessary? What are the consequences?) than with the how and when of it. We are more interested that the man's arm is now genuinely healed than with whether the healing was gradual or instantaneous.

[8] It is important to note here that I have not eliminated any essential teaching of John Wesley's doctrine of Christine Perfection. Historian John L. Peters (*Christian Perfection and American Methodism*, (Grand Rapids: Zondervan, 1987) has summarized Wesley's doctrine of sanctification as follows: (1) it is attainable in this life, and the matter should be pressed; (2) it is limited, involving only the intent and motive of a man; (3) it may be, but need not be lost, since we are never free from temptation; (4) it is both instantaneous and gradual; and (5) the essence of it is perfect love and a walking by faith in the light of God's Word. All of these I affirm with this distinction: that there must be time enough between conversion and sanctification to truly examine one's intent and motive. This view differs from the reformed tradition, in that it still allows for a moment in this life when the believer's heart is finally pure. This view also differs from the Keswick tradition, in that it calls for a total cleansing of the sinful nature, and not merely the suppression of it. Of course, the gradual growth towards sanctification implies a moment when all of it becomes a reality. We will discuss that moment in chapter 10.

[9] Lawrence O. Richards, *The Teacher's Commentary*, (Wheaton: Victor Books, 1987), p. 945.

CHAPTER 8

THOSE DIRTY STAINS

Sin in the Believer's Life

"Those dirty stains."

"You try soaking them out. You try scrubbing them out. You try washing them out. And *still* you come up with . . . ring around the collar."

That was the advertisement jingle for a detergent a few years back. It sold a lot of soap because most of us could identify with it. Everyone knows the frustration of a stubborn stain that won't let go, converting dress shirts into painting smocks for children.

Do you ever wonder if Christ feels the same frustration over the church—whom He loves and desires to present before God "radiant . . ., without stain or wrinkle or any other blemish" (Ephesians 5:27)? He tries scrubbing them out and washing them out, but His children often seem content to wear their righteousness—stained though it may be—out in public, while the public wonders what kind of parent would allow this. Still, God waits patiently for another opportunity to get His children alone, and to scrub the stains one more time, until they are pure at last.

This is a very reasonable hope, one He repeats often in Scripture. And if we will allow the Scriptures to speak for themselves here, we will see the plain teaching of the Bible is that we should not sin any longer, and that if we really don't begin to hate sin with a vengeance, our love for God is not as hot as we say.

In a word, we should learn to hate sin like we would hate the intrusion of another lover in our marriage. We should not enjoy it . . .

coddle it . . .

excuse it . . .

ignore it . . .

arrange it . . .

minimize it . . .

or tolerate it.

The "pleasures of sin," to which all too many evangelicals admit, are for those whose natures have never been cleansed, and whose minds are not fully converted.

It was of particular interest to the Holy Spirit that Job was a man who "feared God and *shunned evil*" (Job 1:1), and it was the advice of Joshua, David, Solomon, Christ, Paul and Peter that we should too.

Yet here is where we struggle. Many are convinced their sins are forgiven, and most will admit the power of sin has been broken. Yet they suffer with a hangover from their former lives, caught in the same cycle—sin, guilt, confession; sin, guilt, confession—until at last they either defect the faith or annex those dirty stains into their definition of what it is to be holy.

Take for example . . .

- the 37-year-old obese woman who keeps eating
  every time she gets nervous. For her, food
  is not a delicacy; it's a sedative. Yet
  she feels conviction for the sin of gluttony.
  Today, she confesses it . . . again. But
  what will happen tomorrow?

- the 16-year-old boy whose sexual passions are
  near their peak. He is prone to fantasies,
  which the camp evangelist has labeled "lust,"
  and now he wants to be sanctified. Can he?
  Will it take his desires away?

- the mother of four children, who cannot control
  her temper and screams when her children
  clutter the house. She really wants to be

the positive, nurturing mother she thinks
all other mothers are, so she asks for this
stubborn stain to be washed away.

- the forty-something victim of substance abuse.
  For years, he's promised his wife he'd quit.
  He's consecrated it a hundred times, and
  believed in faith it was taken away, but
  every other week, it's back with a vengeance.
  What's wrong? Should he bother with holiness?

What do we tell these people? Do we ask them to solve their problems before they sit down to talk about sanctification? Or shall we tell them Jesus will take them as they are, and not to worry about it?

Throughout history, these have been the two extremes in regard to sin in the believer's life. Some, like Count Zinzendorf of the 18th century, have taught that all true believers were entirely sanctified from the first moment of their conversion, and from then on did not sin again. But this is to ignore a central theme in Paul's epistles—that the "still worldly" (1 Corinthians 3:3) are yet "the church of God in Corinth" (1 Corinthians 1:2). They are the same people at the same time. Whether we like it or not, genuine believers can—and sometimes—even often—do sin.

There are others like Augustine, Luther and Calvin who believed we may be saved from the guilt or curse of sin, but never from the power of it. That is, we may break the habits of sin in our lives, but there will always be the seed within us, ready to give rise to more. The trouble with this extreme is that it left only death or purgatory to finish the job of destroying sin in the believer's life. No sane reformer could believe in purgatory (firmly denounced in Luther's 95 theses), so that left only death to provide the magical cure.

"He begins to sanctify us now," wrote Luther in his sermons on the Catechism, "[but] when we have died, he will complete this sanctification . . . ." And again: "When you die . . . then he will raise you up and sanctify you wholly."

By the late 19th century, the Keswick (pronounced without the *w*) doctrine—which held that sin could be suppressed, but never destroyed—provided a safe explanation for many who sided with neither Luther nor Wesley. This "struggle theology," as it has been called, holds that the will of a man may be surrendered, but can never be changed; that is, it will always be more natural for him to do evil than good.[1] In its worst moments, this doctrine has been grossly misunderstood until its proponents fall into a cycle of sin and quiet confession, while they blither away about the flesh being weak. But most who hold to this doctrine are more serious than this about holiness.

Nevertheless, by its insistence that we do *not* have to sin, this doctrine marks a clear departure from early reformed theology (which was more pessimistic about our chances at Christian perfection), and has become the more popular position to hold. Wesleyan historian Melvin Dieter has pointed out that traditional Calvinism in America did not survive its collision with early Methodists of the last century, and so softened its position here to become nearly Keswick. This means that, since the Keswick revival of the late eighteenth century, American Christianity has moved closer to Wesley than ever before. Like Wesley, most now believe sin can be conquered—even for long periods of time. But unlike Wesley, they do not believe it can ever be destroyed.

So these two extremes, *absolute perfectionism* and *struggle theology*, define the ditches on either side of the road toward biblical holiness.

Dialogue with a Bad Theology

These two extremes are often played out in conversation with people who have tried very hard to live above their sin, and having failed many times, decide they will either have to live with their sins or re-label them. Within each extreme, there are two tendencies which often betray themselves in the form of a phrase.

For those who believe they are absolutely perfect, and many of them will never admit to it, there are two tendencies to avoid. The first is to deny sin, and the second is to re-define it.

Deny it

"I don't remember the last time I sinned," a woman said to me recently. Another boasted he had never sinned in more than thirty years. A third admitted to having sinned one time, then added, "but it was a long time ago."

All of this depends on who's looking or to whom they compare themselves. Typically, when the body of Christ stops looking for sin in us, we stop looking for it ourselves. But we must be careful *not* to confuse the last time we sinned with the last time we confessed it. Heaven has its own record of sins committed and sins confessed, and when they are not the same, we are only fooling ourselves. So it is that holy people of the past went looking for them. John Wesley used his solitude to measure himself against the Sermon on the Mount. John of the Cross used, as a plumbline, the seven deadly sins. Martin Luther worked his way through the Ten Commandments. The method or standard we use is less important than the discipline of doing it regularly. Some have pointed out that Paul's own passing from "least of apostles" (1 Corinthians 15:9), to "least of saints" (Ephesians 3:8 KJV), to "chief of sinners" (see 1 Timothy 1:16 KJV) was a process resulting from years of hard self-examination, a discipline he encouraged in his followers.

The danger, of course, is to be morbidly introspective and imagine "sins" which are not real. The best prevention of this is to find a system (such as those above) and then stick with it, admitting to nothing when nothing is present, but seeking a heart of flesh when it is.

Re-define It

Another symptom of a bad theology is when we seek to re-define our sin into a different, lesser category. From those who suffer this malady, we are likely to hear such excuses as "I can't help it . . . that's just the way I am," which are the famous last words of a man about to widen the road to holiness.

Our Catholic brothers are familiar with this in their own theology of *mortal* and *venial* sins. Mortal sins are those huge atrocities like murder, adultery, blasphemy and the like, which cut us off from God and send us to hell. Venial sins are those minor infractions or unforced errors which clutter our love for God, and tie us down. We repent of both, but only the mortal sins can ultimately (although venial sins can lead to mortal sins) hurt us. Of course, there are even Protestant versions of this, in which we slide the sins we hate to love into the "carnality" bracket, and thus label ourselves a "carnal Christian." After this, the sin which so easily entangles us is reduced to a minor infraction, without which we would be so tickled to live, but it cannot hurt us either way. In this way of thinking, the sins I commit before my conversion are sins indeed. Those committed afterwards are "just the way I am." Sin, real sin, is everything we're not and nothing we are.

But remember this: while the "church of God in Corinth" (1 Corinthians 1:2) may be the very ones who are "still worldly" (3:3), they are surely *not* the sexually immoral, nor idolaters, nor adulterers, nor male prostitutes, nor homosexual offenders, nor thieves, nor the greedy, nor drunkards, nor slanderers, nor swindlers whom, we are warned, will never inherit the kingdom of God (see 6:9-10). The idea that we can hide our evil inside the broad confines of "carnal Christian" is a fool's paradise, the very portico of hell.

Another look at the carnal Christians of Corinth will reveal they were guilty of such venial things as "jealousy and quarreling," or the preference of one leader over another (1 Corinthians 3:3-4). Would to God that this (and I do not minimize them) were all that bothered modern Christians who call themselves carnal. Besides, if our carnality in any way makes us more like the Devil than like Christ, there ought to be a holy and restless churning inside us which drives us right to the brink of insanity.

If we are truly the Lord's, "created to be like God in true righteousness and holiness" (Ephesians 4:24), how can we excuse our failures and excesses as temperaments or weaknesses or "rough edges," as though they were the carry-on baggage of our journey? We may, in fact, be righteous—even holy—with these failures, but if we are ever happy with them, or even indifferent toward them, our problem with sin is gigantic. But typically, we will not see this, for "sin is unique," said Catholic theologian Jacques Maritain, "the more we practice it, the less we know of its true nature."

Trivialize it

Within a "struggle theology" there are also a couple of tendencies which sidetrack our pursuit to holiness, ranging from the absurd to the dangerous.

One is to trivialize sin, not by re-defining it, but by acquiescence. From these people, we are likely to hear that "we sin every day in word, thought, or deed." And of course, this depends largely on our definition of sin. While it is true that "all have sinned and fall short of the glory of God" (Romans 3:23), it does not necessarily follow that we *must* sin every day in either word, thought or deed—or several verses have no place in the Bible. Jesus' command to "leave your life of sin" (John 8:11), and John's hope that we "sin not" (1 John 2:1 KJV) are both in vain if we must sin every day—as is John's insistence that "no one who is born of God will continue to sin" (1 John 3:9). And Job's biographer, who had God, himself, call Job "perfect" (Hebrew: *undefiled, blameless*), was misreporting the story.

No. It simply *must* be possible to have for ourselves the kind of virtue we admire in men and women of old, without the kind of vices we only *assume* they had.

Those who believe we must struggle with sin as long as we are in this body of flesh, are usually left with questions more serious than those they thought they answered.

For instance, if sin resides in the flesh, exactly where in the flesh does sin reside?

Did Adam and Eve sin every day in word, thought or deed?

If they did not, why must you?

What did we lose spiritually that God cannot restore?

Is the cure less radical than the disease?

When, after the fall, did God lower His moral expectations?[2]

When did He intend holiness to mean less than what it meant to Adam and Eve?

When will we finally be free from sin? In purgatory or in death?

What power do these have that Christ does not? Is purgatory our Savior? Is death the new covenant? Is death now the ally of Christ and no longer His conquered foe (1 Corinthians 15:57)? If Christ is made Lord in His death, as Luther suggested, then what is the meaning of the Resurrection?

If sin is atoned (or covered), but never defeated, for what do we need the blood of Christ? Why is His blood superior to that of bulls and goats?

True, there are many who sin every day in word, thought or deed, but it is never because they *must*. It is a better epitaph than a theology. It may summarize our lifestyle at the present time, but if we simply accept it, we will collide one day with a God whose expectations will horrify us, whose eye will search out everything . . . and whose holiness we rejected by settling for less.

Tolerate it

Finally, it is possible to tolerate sin, to allow it to move in next door and even spend an evening or two with you. Believe it or not, there are some "Christians" who flirt with disaster by insisting they can do whatever, and God will still forgive them.

As a pastor, I often counsel believers who are unhappy about their marriages and come to seek my help. Often, this is only a thinly veiled way of finding out whether or not they can be forgiven later if they follow through with the sin of divorce today. This "two out of three ain't bad" philosophy misses on several points.

First, it assumes the law of God is an ogre, and not "holy, righteous and good" (Romans 7:12), as Paul said it was. It believes that the Word of God is only a moral restraint, and not an expression of love.

Second, it reveals a lack of desire for holiness. Any faith that seeks to co-exist with sin, knows little about sin and less about holiness, for these are opposite and mutually exclusive virtues. What you give to the one, you take from the other. These people do not desire to be conformed to God's image. They desire to remake Him into their own. And for it, they will find the fires of hell as hot as any other idolater—not for divorce, but for crucifying the Son of God again on the altar of happiness (see Hebrews 6:6).

Third, if Paul was right, he was forgiven because he "acted in ignorance and unbelief" (1 Timothy 1:13), neither of which is an alibi for those who sin in the first degree. During the Middle Ages, certain corrupt priests were making six-figure incomes selling indulgences, which permitted the seeker to sin with forgiveness beforehand. The irony is that Protestants, who once ridiculed the lax faith of their Catholic friends, now find themselves in the same predicament.

Fourth, this premeditated sinning presumes there is no punishment this side of death that is more miserable than the pleasure will be satisfying. And even the consequences after death, it believes, can be put off with a quick prayer of repentance. But as we have already discussed, a repentance that only seeks amnesty, is no repentance at all. These are they who "turn the grace of our God into a license for immorality" (Jude 4), whom we were warned to avoid. They are not of us. And to their own demise, they ignore the law which says they will reap what they sow, and they ignore the stories of Adam, Moses, David and Uzziah which prove it.

Finally, these believers miss entirely the point of conversion. It is for cleansing, and not merely forgiveness, that the truly repentant must cry. And he will seek it whether or not he feels his salvation is gone. Interestingly, even after David sinned with Bathsheba, he was certain he possessed the Holy Spirit (Psalm 51:11), yet he repented anyway, because he was not driven by forgiveness. In fact, there is no hint of David's seeking forgiveness anywhere to be found in the fifty-first Psalm. He wants to be "cleansed" and "washed" (v. 7). He seeks a "pure heart" and a "steadfast spirit" (v. 10), all of which typify holiness and not a mere pardon from impending doom.

Why? Because the goal of repentance is not heaven but holiness. Those who presume upon the grace of God ignore this. All of them need another trip to Isaiah's Temple, where their private little conniptions will melt under the vision of a holy God who stands to fill His temple. A pure vision of God's holiness always magnifies the sin we coddle, and spoils the pleasure of it.

Last year I buried a fairly young woman with cancer, who had a very strange habit about her. When she first suspected she had the disease, she refused to see her doctor, for fear he would confirm it. A year later, when the cancer had reached its final stages, the woman finally admitted it, but still refused to see her physician because now it was "too late."

So last August, fourteen people gathered in a small, quiet chapel to bury a woman, a mother of two, who did not have to die. We knew from those familiar with her case, that a minor surgery early on could have ended the whole sickness.

These then, are the two extremes in our battle with sin. First we deny or redefine it, and then later, when our problem persists, we surrender to it as though it were our lot in life. Meanwhile, God scrubs . . . and washes . . . what we excuse and even cherish.

The Help of Others

It seems to me our whole battle with sin rests on our ability to detect it, and then discipline ourselves against it. In order to **detect** it, we may need to work ourselves through a system of accountability questions with another individual. In one accountability group I was in, we composed a series of affirmations from Psalm 15:

"Who May Live in Your Holy Hill?"

I have lived a blameless life these past few
weeks. Any wrong I may have done was
accidental, or if I knew of it, I quickly confessed
it and felt God's forgiveness. [Those I may
have ignored, you may now tell me. . .]

To the best of my ability, I have loved the
Lord my God with all my soul, heart and mind.
If my mind were a movie, I would feel comfort-
able in watching it together with Christ.

I have been totally honest in my dealings with
other people. I have kept my promises. I have
lived out my vows to my spouse, my children,
and the church [in that order]. My bills are
paid. My obligations are fulfilled.

I have strived to tell the whole truth *in love*.
I have not sacrificed relationships for truth,
nor truth for relationships. I have not gos-
siped nor criticized anyone unfairly.

I have hated evil, and refused to tolerate,
rationalize, or compromise it wherever

I have seen it, whether in my life or the
environment around me.

I have been partial to my fellow believers,
seeking to encourage them and support them
whenever I could.

I have tithed faithfully and cheerfully. I
have spent my money for the glory of God and
the advance of His kingdom. I have resisted
materialism, and am content with my income.

This is a good habit to get into, primarily because the God with
whom we deal may ask us these questions, whether we ask them of
ourselves or not. And even if we must wait years for that day to come,
the mere passage of time between now and then means nothing to Him
who is timeless.

We may also need to **discipline** ourselves to ask the second
question: not *what* sin did we commit, but rather *why* did we commit it?
This will expose the sin behind the sin, which we discussed in chapter 3.
We must then confess these things one to another that we may be healed
(James 5:16). For our private sins are like vampires, they lose their
power when we expose them to the light of others.

Learn to Love First

Yet underneath our resolve to detect and discipline the sin in our
lives, we must possess a love for God, a fascination with His character,
a profound respect for His holiness, a passion to imitate Him. For this
is the most fundamental component to overcoming sin. The faithful
husband does not commit adultery, not because he fears divorce, but
because he truly loves his wife. The holy Christian does not continue to
sin, not because he fears punishment, but because he loves his God.

"True holiness consists in having but one fear, the loss of God's
friendship," wrote the great saint, Gregory of Nyssa, in the fourth century.

It is the same today. And the moral here is that whatever we do to
sin in our lives, we must learn to love God first. For if we do, we will
find those things which entangle us beginning to lose their grip.

But this is not the way holiness is preached at first.

"Is sanctification a requirement or optional?" we ask.

It's a bad question, but the most common answer is worse: "It is an
absolute requirement, it is the will of God for you to be sanctified." And

by the time we have rattled off the references to prove it, we have made entire sanctification the eleventh commandment, or a legalistic requirement, which is not what God intended.

To be sure, holiness is the logical conclusion of a decent conversion. But where is the power of love? Imagine the look of horror on the face of a new bride when her husband turns to ask, "Now that we're married, do we have to be intimate?"

What fool would marry someone whom he could not love? Marriage is not merely changing our marital status in the courts. It is acknowledging before the public our love for another person and our desire to spend the rest of our lives with them. In similar fashion, holiness is not merely the changing of our status in heaven, it is acknowledging our love for God and our desire to become more and more after the image of Him, whom we say we love. It is an ever-increasing oneness, prompted by love.

So when we seek to loosen the sins which cling to us, we must deal first, not with the sins themselves, but with our level of love for God. For we are not sanctified the way we were saved. In our conversion, we were driven or pushed into repentance by a deep conviction or guilt over having broken the rules (Galatians 3:24). In sanctification, we are pulled or compelled by a holy fascination to become one again with the Father and to bear His image.

When we are pushed towards sanctification only by a desire to get rid of certain sins, we will not have holiness, but morality. The trouble with "consecrationists" (those who believe we need only consecrate that *one sin* entangling us) is that, in their haste to get us sanctified, they forget the power of love.

For years, I struggled with the same sin. Every time I heard a sermon on laying aside the sin which so easily entangles us (see Hebrews 12:1), the message was telegraphed right to me. The preacher never had to list the sins. I knew which one he meant. This one sin was a sort of troll guarding the bridge to sanctification. So, at the end of every other sermon, I would hotfoot it down to the altar to consecrate myself to God—not because I wanted holiness, but because I wanted to conquer that one sin. Consecration was the short version of an otherwise slow and tedious process of "put[ing] to death the misdeeds of the body" (Romans 8:13), and "learning to say 'No' to ungodliness" (see Titus 2:12). Then days later, when I would find myself stumbling into the same pattern, I blamed the grace of God for not taking my sin away. I was looking for the quick kill of a sin that I, myself, was supposed to strangle myself. While I prayed, "God, help me"—I meant "make it easy." And it never was.

My private sin was only conquered when I was compelled by

Christ's love to shed it myself.

One fable tells the story of a contest between the sun and the wind, to remove the coat from a man walking down a path. The wind went first, and whipped up a storm strong enough to blow the overcoat off the man. But as the wind grew stronger, the man clung more tightly to his overcoat until, at last, the wind gave up. Now it was the sun's turn. With a bright glow, it heated the day until the temperature became warmer and warmer, and the man—all by himself—removed his coat to enjoy the warmth of the sun.

If we are to remove those stubborn sins which have wrapped themselves around us, we cannot simply blast them off in an instant with high-powered sermons or high-pressure invitations. We must allow the love of God to shed itself abroad in our hearts until there is precious little room left for anything else.

"If you love me," Jesus said, "you will obey what I command" (John 14:15). And since it is always possible to obey whom we truly love (but never the other way around), we must learn to love first.

Dear Christian, get to know God.

Study Him.

Talk to Him.

Laugh with Him.

Pace the floor and think with Him.

It is not the deeper life you crave, but God, himself. And once you have found Him, you will hardly notice the stains you are missing.

NOTES:

[1] H.W. Webb-Paploe, a dominant figure in early Keswick Conventions (1875), summarized this doctrine: "I have found that . . . (grace) does not deliver me from the perpetual instigation and presence of evil, and the principle of sin, the indwelling natural tendency and taste which once came from Adam, and which, I believe, remains somewhere in the being of man to the last." Another early Keswick writer, Evan Hopkins, said that "sanctification, in the sense of a definite decision for holiness . . . is a crisis," while the attainment of Christian Perfection itself is "a gradual process, a continuous process, an endless process." See Herbert F. Stevenson, *Keswick's Authentic Voice: Sixty-Five Dynamic Addresses Delivered at the Keswick Convention, 1875-1957*, (Grand Rapids: Zondervan, 1959), pp. 31-40, and 332-337. More recently, Keswick theologian J.R. McQuilken speaks of an ongoing "conflict . . . between the old nature and the indwelling Holy Spirit," and says that in conversion "a new life-force has nature." To McQuilken, the sinful disposition itself is never converted, but only suppressed with an antidote of faith and the Holy Spirit. See J.R. McQuilken, *Five Views on Sanctification*, (Grand Rapids: Zondervan, 1987), pp. 151-183.

[2] The distinction "moral expectations" is important here. Wesley separated the fallen man's moral image from his *natural image* (which provided for him immortality, understanding and free will), and his *political image* (which provided

his right and reason to govern the earth). To Wesley, the *moral image* was comprised of those moral attributes of God (he cites love and purity as examples) given to men at creation. While Christian Perfection would surely improve a man's understanding and ability to rule the earth, the primary focus of it was on his moral image, which could be restored to its original condition before the fall. See Wesley's sermon, "The New Birth," *The Works of John Wesley*.

CHAPTER 9

IT'S ALL IN YOUR HEAD

The Sanctification of the Mind

They're fighting again in the Middle East.

Only this time, everyone's watching. Modern satellites and "live coverage" reporting make it possible these days to watch a war while it is happening.

It's the ultimate in interactive video. First we watch. Then we "play along" by putting pressure on kings and generals who, all the while hating the media, must play to its worldwide audience. History's Hitlers and Husseins can no longer thumb their nose at the world, because now the world can see them. Suddenly, even the worst of them feels obligated to explain his actions away in the presence of one measly news correspondent. But all of this has its limits, as one journalist reported recently: "While the city is enjoying peace under the watchful eye of TV reporters and UN peacekeepers," he said, "thousands of crimes and atrocities go unseen in smaller, rural areas where no one is looking. And this is the real battle."

Fascinating! We can clean up any neighborhood by broadcasting its atrocities in front of the world, but long after the last spectator has turned off the television, the real battle rages in places the world will never see.

What's true of life is true of conversion. It seems only moments after a man's conversion, all of the attention is directed towards his lifestyle. What is he doing? Who are his friends? What places does he frequent? What music does he play? What slang does he use?

These are the parts of him we broadcast before the Christian world. And pity the poor soul who does not clean them up. He will never have a moment's rest.

But like any war, long after the last spectator in the church has stopped looking, the real battle rages in a place the world will never see: *the mind*!

Religion's Last Frontier

"Sow a thought, and you reap an act," goes the adage.
"Sow an act, and you reap a habit."
"Sow a habit and you reap a character."
"Sow a character and you reap a destiny."
But it all begins with a thought.

Actually, it isn't quite that simple, but it's close. Everything begins in the mind. In fact, Martin Luther argued it was impossible to sin without first thinking wrongly about God. In this sense, our mind is the origin of evil.

It is also the final resting place. For once our evil thought has been translated into an action, it is broadcast to the watching world. And once the action has been soundly condemned, it is too often never eliminated, but pushed back into the mind where no one, including the guilty, can see it. It's the invisible sin that kills us. For that which is not seen is usually not confessed. And sin that is unconfessed is forever free to carry on its campaign against the soul. So the Devil will ruin us with our sin, if he can only keep it out of our lifestyle and stuck in our minds.

That he has at least somewhat succeeded, is evident from the dichotomy modern Christians have made between their brain and their body. Sin does not seem to be sin unless it is acted upon.

"You hated her, didn't you?" says the attorney to the man accused of murdering his boss.

"Yes, and I *still* hate her," admits the defendant, "but I didn't kill her." And the jury finds him innocent.

But in the courts of heaven, he is guilty. For Jesus condemned hatred and murder, lust and adultery, pride and idolatry, fear and unbelief to the same fires.

It is true for some of us that our conversions did not go far enough. Perhaps in our "conversion," the demons which once racked our soul, merely fled to our mind, and then for want of renewal, repossessed our soul with a greater vengeance than before (Matthew 12:29, 43-45). The purpose of this chapter is to explore this vast and final frontier of the mind, and to measure the claims of holiness upon it. We will conclude, I hope, with practical advice concerning its sanctification. For when all is said and done, *it's all in your head.*

The Two Disciplines of the Mind

In the sanctification of the mind, there are two disciplines we must develop: the more difficult is that of (1) *transforming the mind,* but the more immediate is (2) the *captivating of every thought.* Now these two disciplines work in tandem, so it is practically useless to have one without the other. Unless we can captivate our thoughts, there is no point in trying to transform the overall condition of our mind, for any harmless and passing thought can have a fatal attraction.

The opposite is also true. Any attempt to captivate our thinking must be met with an equal effort to transform the whole mind, since this is the origin and final resting place for every thought. The tragedy of a shallow faith is that it merely puts a lid over our evil thoughts without purifying the source from which they perpetually flow. This is sometimes evident in those whose minds have weakened with age.

Peculiarly, it is often those who were the most "religious" in their early years, that become the most lurid towards the end. This is especially true of those for whom legalism has been a way of life. It is true of some that once their mouths become unguarded, their minds simply empty themselves of whatever was in them all along. The swearing, lying, and filthy language are the mental wreckage of a life that has focused only on captivating the thought but never transforming the mind. And later, when the mind is too weak to captivate anything, the old ghosts return with a vengeance. Colossians says the legalists' "regulations indeed have an appearance of wisdom . . . but they lack any value in restraining sensual indulgence" (2:23).

So let's look at these two disciplines in more detail.

Transforming the Mind

When Augustine said, "It takes only a minute to convert the soul but a lifetime to convert the mind," he meant the transformation process. This is the process in which we gradually absorb the mind of Christ, including His values, disposition, reasoning and imaginations. Simply put, we think the way Christ does.

The Hope

Those who deny this is even possible ought to consider the way lifetime lovers gradually develop the very mind, even personality of their spouse over the years. This is no freak occurrence. It happens thousands of times every year all over the world. Skeptics ought to wonder why it is they accept one definition of intimacy for their marriages, and another for their religion; and why it is they usually wind up loving their spouses (in whose image they were *not* made) much more than their God (in whose image they *were* made).

And they ought to examine again what Paul meant when he prayed for all Christians everywhere to have a "love that surpasses knowledge" (Ephesians 3:19), or when he charged one church to "let this mind be in you which was also in Christ Jesus" (Philippians 2:5 KJV), and went on to describe Christ's best moments and not His worst. They should wonder again for what Christ was praying when He asked to be one with His disciples like He was one with the Father (John 17:21-23). All of this means *something*, doesn't it?

The hope of God is that we would have much more of His mind than we are currently settling for. And when we are tempted to think it is some ethereal state, unlike anything we know or could even identify, we should ask why Christ prayed for it in the past perfect tense, and how it is Paul, himself, believed "we have the mind of Christ" (1 Corinthians 2:15).

The bottom line is that we, who are so natural at thinking one way, must learn to think another.

Dr. Paul Brand, the missionary-surgeon to India, illustrates this process beautifully by using an analogy of leprosy patients who seek reconstructive surgery for parts of their bodies once ravaged by the disease.

> We give some leprosy patients new eyebrows [for
> cosmetic purposes] by cutting a swatch of hairy
> scalp and tunneling it under the forehead to the
> eyebrow area. It comes still attached to the
> scalp's original nerve and blood supply, and so
> the patient's eyebrows still "feel like" part of
> his scalp. If a fly crawls across the transplanted

eyebrow, the patient will likely respond by
slapping his crown. Or, in a tendon transfer
procedure I may move a healthy tendon from the
ring finger to the thumb. . . "move your thumb,"
I will say, and nothing happens. The patient
just stares at his hand. "Now move your ring
finger," I say, and the thumb springs forward.[1]

Dr. Brand says, "The patient must repattern his or her brain" for the
procedure to do any lasting good.

"It can take months to reestablish smooth patterns," he says, "and
many over the age of forty never fully adjust to the change."

This is the process of transformation. And for the believer, there is
no other way to transform the mind than to reprogram it after the fashion
of Scripture.

Why? Because *our minds will never be more holy than our
knowledge of Scripture will allow.* So he is no friend of God who
ignores God's Word. For the Word of God has always been the solvent
He uses to wash His people (Ephesians 5:26). How can anyone *in* Christ
want it any other way?

The Obstacle

Yet, while I write, the rates for illiteracy in my country are sky-
rocketing far beyond the dangerous, into the absurd. According to one
five-year government study, completed in 1991, over 90 million
Americans cannot read well enough to complete their assignments at
work. Another study just released from the National Assessment
Governing Board indicates that only one-third of all 12th graders in this
country are proficient readers. Small wonder the average newspaper is
written for the fourth grade, and the Bibles which sell the most today are
geared for sixth graders and under. And even then, they are largely
ignored by their proud owners. Most of what modern Americans gain in
terms of biblical insight are the product of sermons, and not the reward
of mining the Scriptures for themselves. And if theologian David Wells
is right, Scripture-less sermons are the worst kept secret in the church
today.

"Only 19.5 percent [of sermons in evangelical churches today] were
grounded in or related in any way to the nature, character and will of
God," said Wells. Now since the "nature, character and will of God" are
not just topics within the Scripture, but the very essence of it, one could
reasonably argue that many preachers today preach "Scripture-less"
sermons from the Scripture. The pulpit presumes on the pew, and the

pew on the pulpit, until neither side is reading the Bible much these days. In one holiness church I visited recently, I counted five Bibles coming through the door, none of which were opened while the message was read. But then, we were never asked to open them, either.

Those believers who *can* read often waste what little literacy they have on books which will occupy the clearance rack in a year. Their Bibles, as fancy as they are ignored, do everything but read themselves to the poor souls who neglect them in deference to the latest literary insight into raising their kids or planning their retirement.

Dear Christian, if you only read one book this year, *put this one down*. And in the name of God, go back to the Bible. It is God's first choice. Anything else, including this book, is plan-B.

The Goal

As we begin to reprogram our minds, we must remember that the goal of all this is to get ourselves to reason and think in ways that are parallel to the Bible. It is to think Christianly. It is to do the right thing and to know why. We want to build Scriptural parameters around our thoughts so they can never stray too far. We want the Bible to be the first point considered, and the last left standing when the argument is over— as it was for Christ in the wilderness. We want to learn to interpret life by the Scriptures, and not the other way around, so our lives become an illustration of the truth. We want to look through the Word of God to watch the news, budget our money, chart the future—even select the entertainment for the evening. We want to feel its truth in times of crisis.

This, and not the mere memorization of it, is what Wesley meant when he committed himself to become "*homo unius libri*—a man of one book—regarding none, comparatively, but the Bible."[2] But we must remember that this is a discipline—a bath and not a brainwashing.

The Process

How do we do this? For the already-converted, the best way to enter the Bible is through **repentance** for not having come here before. Let us begin by admitting we do not already have a transformed mind. However humiliating it may be, let's confess sloth of a lazy mind that runs in any direction as easily as water into ditches.

Let us admit that we simply cannot transform the mind on five-minute devotionals or Christian radio or thought-for-the-day calendars. Would to God that His people were as literate about Paul as they are their favorite radio preacher.

Let us tell ourselves the truth: that God cares very little how busy we are, even with good pursuits, if we are always too busy for Him.

Let us repent of our addiction to the amphetamine of activity, as if it were the hallmark of a VIP. Let us acknowledge our compulsion to read our mail (which is temporal) more faithfully than our Bibles (which is eternal).

Let us confess our failure to take God's Word seriously as the horrible sin that it is. It is true of many, at least in my day, that whatever morals they possess, they did not find them for themselves in the Bible. They are the hollow and powerless hand-me-downs of the last generation. So we must convince ourselves that God, who has been trying to get through to us, is probably not much more impressed with a moral illiterate than with an immoral one.

Why start here? Because repentance is the most effective method to bring about lasting change. Any attempt at reading the Bible intensively is destined to fail after a few short weeks, unless it is founded on repentance for having neglected it already up to this time. We must be sincere. We cannot begin studying the Bible because our pastor told us to, or because we read this chapter, or because our spouses complained about not having family devotions. These may get us started, but they cannot keep us going.

Now there is nothing mystical about learning the Bible and incorporating it. We learn the Bible the way we learn a new word in our vocabulary: we read it, memorize it, and use it in a sentence.

(1) *Read it.* As painfully obvious as this may seem, it is a vastly neglected discipline today. But there is good reason for it, as I learned from one young lady in my congregation.

"Could you recommend a good book to help me understand Genesis?" she asked. "But it has to be really simple."

So I recommended one. In fact, I gave her my copy. A week later she returned, saying she didn't understand it.

"That's too complicated for me," she said, "got another one?" So I gave her the simplest of the simple. And when she returned it a week later, pronouncing it a total failure, I grew suspicious and asked what part of Genesis she couldn't understand.

"I don't know," she said with a straight face, "I haven't read it yet."

To her, the Bible couldn't be that simple if there were so many books out there to help her understand it.

She has a point. My last stroll through the Christian bookstore turned up 60 translations, 40 study Bibles, and 36 books to help me study it for myself. All of this aside from the usual smattering of reference tools and commentaries, now too numerous to mention.

Most of these are written with the vision of helping the young fledgling gain a basic understanding of the Bible. But far too often, these have the opposite effect by making us so dependent upon the "study helps" that we can hardly imagine ourselves getting anything worthwhile out of the Bible without the handy notes of a "scholar" somewhere nearby.

A very famous professor of literature was once asked the best way to understand Shakespeare.

"Read Shakespeare," he said.

So, read Genesis. Read the whole Bible. Underline it. Write your comments in the margins. But the idea here is consistency and variety. It is more important that you read it regularly than that you read it for a long time. And it is more important that you expose your mind to a *broad variety* of Scripture than it is that you become an expert on any one passage or book. Allow God to speak to you through the law, the prophets, the Psalms, the gospels and the epistles. Yes, even Leviticus and Revelation. And as you read, ask yourself two questions: (1) What does this passage tell me about God?; and (2) What does it tell me about what it means to be the people of God?

You will find the Bible has a wonderful capacity to reveal, not only the righteousness of God, but your own hidden motives as well (Psalm 19:12). Like a good, steady downpour of rain, the Scripture will not create the holes in the roof, but it will surely find them.

(2) *Memorize it.* It is one of the suspicious ironies of our day that people who memorize recipes and batting averages cannot memorize the Bible. Modern psychology's latest discovery that there isn't such a thing as a bad memory—only a lazy one—is especially indicting to those who have relied on a "bad memory" for years. The lights have come on to reveal their nakedness. The truth is, most people who really *try* to memorize the Bible, can, and those who go through the trouble, find the Bible portable and compact. They can plug it into any conversation or quandary without having to read chapter and verse. The wisdom of God becomes usable in places where a Bible-in-hand would be clumsy or snap the power of a teachable moment. It is like knowing the key to your computer as opposed to looking up each command in the manual.

What is more, a treasure house of memory is the raw material of meditation. Simply put, we rarely meditate on verses we have not memorized first. And it is only through meditation—the mauling of a verse over and over in our minds—that we become anything like what we have just read.

"Those who pass too rapidly from one truth to another feed their curiosity and restlessness," wrote the mystic Francois Fenelon, who encouraged us to "give every truth time to send down deep roots into the heart."

Two hundred years later, the Scottish preacher, Maurice Roberts agreed.

It is not the busy skimming over religious books or the careless hastening through religious duties which makes for a strong Christian faith. Rather it is unhurried meditation on gospel truths and the exposing of our minds to these truths that yields the fruit of sanctified character.[3]

(3) *Use it in a sentence.* This is the real bottleneck. In most congregations, there are literally hundreds of verses which have been added to the collective memory of the church, but which do the people little good because they have never been taken off the proverbial shelf and put to good use. In many cases, the last time the memory verse is ever heard is when it is recited in exchange for a prize. And all of this is a happy hunting ground for the Devil, who cares very little how many verses we know, so long as we are afraid or unable to use them.

So take them down, and implement those verses on the shelf. You can do this by journaling your thoughts about a passage you may have read. Or by incorporating them into your testimonies. Or read the Bible and change your mind about something, and then explain to others why you did so. Or teach a children's class, which will force you to articulate your verses into a plan of action. Or write practical, lifechange articles for a newsletter, which weaves these once-shelved verses into the fabric of contemporary thought.

In short, we reprogram the mind like any ordinary computer. First we store the verses on the hard drive (memory), then call them forward from the hard drive and into the random access memory where we can do something with them. Here we meditate on them awhile, and afterwards send them back to the hard drive, until it is so possessed that even when our mind seems to be in neutral, it defaults to the mind of Christ.

Captivating Every Thought

The second, and more immediate discipline of the mind, is that of controlling our thoughts. Every verse we memorize, every prayer we say, every sermon we hear will be plundered of its power if we are not faithful in this matter of "[taking] captive every thought [and making] it obedient to the lordship of Christ" (2 Corinthians 10:5).

There are a few ways to do this. The most obvious is *the discipline of avoiding people or situations which stimulate our thoughts and raise themselves up against the mind of Christ.*

- We cannot realistically expect to sit in front of a television for very long without learning to need something we really don't.

- We cannot meander past the skin magazines or sift through the literary pornography of a romance novel for too long without desiring a little of it for ourselves, and soon afterwards becoming dissatisfied with our own marriage.
- We cannot soak our minds in the rebellious lyrics of some music without sooner or later resenting those in authority over us.
- We cannot sit in circles with our friends, and roast the character of other people over the open fires of slander and criticism without very soon thinking more highly of ourselves than we ought.
- We cannot watch the violence and the carnage of Hollywood without imagining a little vengeance for ourselves.

Another of the tragic ironies today is that many who fight hard to protect their environment from toxins, and their bodies from viruses, should naively assume they can expose their minds to anything they desire without it having any effect whatsoever on their thought life. Poor fools. They do not know that we contract an evil thought in much the same way we contract a common cold—by exposure.

If we are honest with ourselves for a moment, we will see that much of the warfare we have with our mind is waged against thoughts that were once invited, nurtured, armed and patronized by ourselves. Said the comic strip character Pogo: "We have met the enemy, and he is us."

Aside from this, however, is the arduous task of captivating the innocent wanderings of the mind when it is in neutral. Unfortunately, the mind still runs, even when we are not running it. Almost without warning, it slips up the antenna and begins scanning for something on which to dwell. And before we know, we are fighting the battle again.

"It is not the heavy thinking that shapes our characters," wrote A.W. Tozer, "but the quiet attention of the mind to the surrounding world day after day throughout our lives."

Translated, that means it is not just the man sitting in front of the TV beer commercials who is in harm's way. It's the guy sitting at the cafeteria during the lunch break, or the one listening to easy rock radio during the half-hour trek to work each morning. It's the mother staring blankly out the window as she rocks the baby. Or the couple making conversation as they wait for dinner to be served. It's the man in the boat waiting for the fish to bite, or the woman jogging in the late afternoon, or the high schooler with no assignments during study hall.

"The human mind—left unattended—will run to mischief as quickly as a garden runs to weeds," wrote Tozer. And so it is imperative we captivate *every* thought—not just the bad ones—and make those thoughts obedient to Christ.

Practical Suggestions

A few suggestions may help us here. One is to **watch and pray**. This suggestion is based on the assumption that strength is not as vulnerable to disease as is weakness. Perhaps this is why Christ tied the discipline of prayer to "not fall[ing] into temptation" (Luke 22:46). Perhaps He saw evil as something to be resisted and not merely overcome. To Him, prayer was an inoculation and not an antibiotic. Even so, I have found a strong connection between my resistance and whatever the temperature of my spiritual life at the time. Whether or not I can meet and resist temptation is largely dependent upon the momentum I have gathered up to that point. For the amount of power an evil thought possesses usually runs in inverse proportion to the amount of power *I* possess when I am first tempted. So if I am wise, I will learn to shore up my defenses during the in-between times by— once again, bathing them in the Word of God.

A second suggestion is to **substitute one thought for another**, or as Paul put it, to "overcome evil with good" (Romans 12:21). When I share this concept with an audience, I ask them to think of any number between one and ten, but *not* to think of the number three. After driving that forbidden number deep into their minds, I ask them to tell me the number they've chosen, and then whether or not they were tempted to think of three. Naturally, most of them were.

This illustrates a fundamental principle: we do not rid our minds of evil thoughts by telling ourselves *not* to think them. We only eliminate evil when we displace it with something else. If you don't want to wrestle with the number three, then begin by thinking of seven. If you don't want to wrestle with evil, begin by thinking of good. One alternative is to think of two people you know who are unusually talented and influential, and each time you're tempted with an evil thought, begin to pray for these two by name—that God would either convert or sanctify them for His use. In this way, you will be replacing the evil thought with the "good" of praying for others.

One man who confessed to the sin of lust, admitted he spent the first month or two praying continually, and after that, began to cast the evil out for the first time in his life.

A third suggestion is to **tell yourself the truth**. Since most of our evil thoughts are based on a fantasy or lie, they will evaporate like fog in the hot sun, the very moment we expose them to the truth.

So before we get carried away with the thought, we might as well acknowledge that we're *never* going to possess all that we want (which is greed). We're *not* going to meet that imaginary lover in private (which is lust). We're *not* going to bring our enemies to their knees (which is vengeance). We're *not* going to win the standing ovation of those we are trying to impress (which is pride). And the real truth is that we don't want these things anyway. We want the feelings of peace, significance, and satisfaction we think these things will bring us. But these are only found when the soul and mind lose themselves in God, who will come nowhere near these sins. These things are not the shortcut to happiness. They are more of a necessary detour. And the sooner we tell ourselves the truth, the less time we will waste with them.

This final suggestion has tremendous power: *confess our thoughts one to another.* Our relationship with others will sink a mile deeper the moment we are honest. Our friendships will become stronger and more authentic as those to whom we confess our sins, in turn, confess nearly the same ones back to us (after all, people of a similar age often share the same temptations). Then together, we can celebrate our gains and compensate for our losses.

If nothing else, the sheer intimidation of knowing we are going to be asked again about our impure thoughts is nearly enough to scare them right out of us. So let us choose our partners carefully, then "confess [our] sins one to another that we may be healed" (James 5:16).

A Parable

I hate to garden, but I have one.

In fact, I work it every day. Planting and pulling and carefully cultivating seeds I have sown.

Most of this is done when no one else is around. I just sneak it in during the after-hours of the day, and even during the free times at work. Times when I'm not otherwise occupied. You might say it's a private matter.

I seldom talk about my garden, and when other gardeners ask how it's doing or what I'm growing, I usually mutter something like "Ah . . . the general stuff." Which means the same stuff you're growing.

That is, I'm growing some things I like and some things I don't. Don't ask me why. I haven't completely figured that out. I often grow what I do not remember planting, and tell myself I'll know whether I want it or not when it blooms. But by that time it's usually too late. What can you do with it?

I've also noticed it is more difficult growing the things I like than those I don't. I've blamed it on any number of things these past few years, but I'm beginning to concede it must be the soil.

Then there are the weeds. They're the tough part of this job. I'm never sure how to handle them. Another gardener of a different era offered me this advice: "It is not enough to love flowers," he said, "you must also hate weeds." I think he's right.

But what about the weeds that sprout flowers? I have this love-hate relationship with them. So sometimes I let them grow. And they grow quickly. And spread? Wow! It's unbelievable. I wish the good stuff I planted would grow that fast. But then, nothing worthwhile ever does. Anyway, for awhile, I gardened these flowery weeds (if you can call it gardening), but before long I noticed they were strangling some of the good things I planted and began to ruin the appearance of my garden.

So I started uprooting these attractive, but pesky weeds. Don't think *that* was easy. There were days I wanted to surrender the whole garden, converting it over to the maintenance-free weeds. But I remembered winter was coming. That would be a day of reckoning. I would be able to use the fruit but not the weeds. So I plodded on.

Since then I have observed many other gardeners who share the same struggles and yet the same desires that I do. And I have witnessed that those who carefully tend to their gardens are the happiest and most well-adjusted people in the world. And I have sought to study and learn from them.

They have taught me to choose my crop rather than to take a chance on what might come up one day. And never to plant or cultivate any fruit that might embarrass me later. They have encouraged me to attack the problem of weeds (even the flowery ones) early and often. They say it's easier to maintain a good, clean garden than to recover one that has run to weeds. I suspect they're right.

I have seen their struggles, and I am convinced that in the end, all of their sweat and hard work and sacrifice paid off. Even during the hardest seasons when they were paying the price, they were, all the while, reaping the benefits. So I think of them each time I get mesmerized by weeds and want to surrender my garden to the course of least resistance.

I think of another Friend, too. He's a great Gardener, the best in the world. A legend in these matters. They say He planted only the things He wanted and never tolerated anything less. I've even read somewhere that He never had so much as a single weed appear in His garden . . . ever! But I know He worked it all the time.

Nevertheless, He is always willing to stroll with me through mine (actually, He is more willing than welcome) and point out the good fruit and the bad.

And weeds? Does He ever know weeds! He is never fooled by their flowers or innocence. He seems to look straight into the future and see the day when they will overrun the whole garden. It's my guess He's seen it before. But He never plucks them out for me. He simply *points* them out and leaves the decision to me.

Many times I mistake Him for a fruit inspector. But I have seen a love in His eyes over the past few years, and I can say He is more than that. He is a Gardener. And His first interest is . . . no, not gardens or even fruit . . . but gardeners like me.

Personally, I'm not much for gardening. But I love this Gardener. And if for no other reason than that—and that is reason enough—I choose this day to tend to my garden.

NOTES:

[1] Dr. Paul Brand and Philip Yancey, *In His Image*, (Grand Rapids: Zondervan, 1984), p. 146.

[2] His own words in John Wesley, *Entire Sanctification, Attainable in This Life*, reprint of *Plain Account*, (Salem: H.E. Schmul), p. 13.

[3] Cited by Donald Whitney in *Spiritual Disciplines of the Christian Life*, (Colorado Springs: NavPress, 1991), p. 51.

CHAPTER 10

CRISIS?
WHAT CRISIS?

When and How to be Entirely Sanctified

Among the many casualties inflicted on the public by the advertising industry of our day is an insidious skepticism that everything available is somehow overrated.

Nothing is free.

You can't have it all.

Nothing is as good as it seems.

This has become the cynical disposition of our culture in which "words have gone wild," as Henri Nouwen said in the early 1980s. Quite simply: the more we talk, the less we mean. This is especially true in advertising.

The bait-n-switch commercial artists have us flat worn out, as nearly everyone knows. Just this week, I was offered a chance to

    . . . buy a European import for $299 a month, or

    . . . select any five CDs for only 99 cents, or

    . . . get 10 *free* hours of online service.

That's what the large print said anyway. But like you, I have noticed a fine print that is much longer and farther away from the original offer, and is considerably less optimistic. In most cases, I do not qualify for these consumer bonanzas. And even when I do, "certain restrictions apply." So the advertisement giveth, and the fine print taketh away.

This attitude has become so common that most of us have simply come to expect less, until we learn to distrust the advertisements, and then later ignore them altogether. My glamorous opportunities to own the European Import, the five CDs, or the ten hours of online service are all sitting in the dumpster, next to the dozens of other offers I never bothered to read.

With this in mind, it shouldn't surprise us that the gospel has fallen on hard times ever since we began to peddle it in the 1960s. For any religion that is designed to meet the needs of one particular culture will probably promise far more than it can deliver. It *must*, just in order to keep up with all of the other "products" out there in our oversell society.

Nevertheless, the real gospel is still available to any and every man. And genuine holiness, without which no man will see the Lord, is available to every believer. Moses' humility, David's heart after God, Paul's pressing toward the mark, Augustine's "give me what Thou will," Wesley's heart strangely warmed, or Mother Teresa's one holy passion are not so extraordinary, as they are the right use of grace made available to all of us at one time or another. God neither supplies nor expects less for any man.

But sadly, most of us would rather envy these saintly heroes than imitate them. We would rather believe it came easier for them than for us, or that God has designed a secret caste system inside His kingdom, and made it virtually impossible for anyone to penetrate a level other than the one they already occupy.

All of this talk about holiness is overrated, we say. Certain restrictions apply. And so we (and there are plenty of us) who once believed we were the exceptions, have made ourselves the rule, and settled ourselves in to a foolish assumption that there is safety in numbers.

But one day, and typically after we are dead, we will learn that heaven is far more serious about holiness, and much more sophisticated about heart purity than most of us are down here. And in the meantime, we still have to confront the Scriptures, which say that . . .

. . . Christ has come to give us life more abundantly (John 10:10), and that He later prayed for our sanctification (John 17:19).

. . . God has ordained, from the very beginning, that we should be "conformed to the likeness of his Son" (Romans 8:29).

. . . we were chosen "to be holy and blameless in his sight" (Ephesians 1:4), and to "share in his holiness" (Hebrews 12:10).

. . . God "did not call us to be impure, but to live a holy life"

(1 Thessalonians 4:7).

. . . He is "able to do immeasurably more than all we ask or imagine" (Ephesians 3:20).

. . . we should, each of us, offer our bodies as living sacrifices, "holy and pleasing to God—[which is our] spiritual act of worship" (Romans 12:1).

These are not for other men. They are for *us*. And they are all we think they are . . . and more! And in this chapter, we want to look specifically at how we may have them for ourselves.

The Crisis of Sanctification

We have been saying that sanctification (or "complete devotion" as we called it in chapter 7) is possible in this life, but does not necessarily happen just because we consecrate ourselves. It is not only more of commitment that leads to a crisis of entire sanctification, but less of sin and selfishness as well. It can happen, but it usually takes longer than we think.

My generation, at least, has seen a multitude of holiness folk who prayed to receive "the blessing," as it was called, but who never then rid themselves of habits and attitudes indigenous to their former, sinful life. They were just as stingy or cantankerous as any old cuss, only now they had a testimony.

You might say the children of today have decided that if it doesn't quack like a duck, fly like a duck or swim like a duck, then it isn't a duck—whether it says so or not. The sanctified-by-intimidation demeanor of the past has left a sour taste in our mouths. And for years we wanted nothing to do with the doctrine of holiness. But at last we have begun to separate the gift from its vendors, and now we want it again.

Only we want the real thing. We have learned that much of the "touch not, taste not, handle not" paraphernalia associated with sanctification has precious little, in reality, to do with the Holy Spirit who allegedly inspired it. So with or without the rules; with or without the circus of emotion; with or without the fire-breathing evangelists; and with or without the made-for-television testimonies, the sons of this modern age, like their godly predecessors who were honest with themselves, desire a life wholly devoted to the glory of God alone. We want sanctified careers and marriages too. We want pure minds that meditate, more than covet or lust. We want hearts without carnal ambitions. And we want temples suited for the dwelling of Christ. But we are not so interested in how high one jumps at the altar, as in how he walks when he finally comes down.

So how are we sanctified? There are three steps or stages. We must (1) wait on God; we must (2) seize the moment; and we must (3) reform our lifestyle. And *always* in this order.

Wait On God

In a culture of fast food, automatic tellers, 150 megahertz, and "I-want-it-yesterday" deadlines, the suggestion to "wait" has become a dirty four-letter word. So it is not coincidence that consecration and altar-call conversions were developed in my country during the same time as the industrial revolution. Formula and mass production were the new language of the early 19th century. And the church was manufacturing converts (step one, step two, step three. . .) the way Eli Whitney had been manufacturing cotton since 1796. Not all of this was bad, of course. It really did call, and then settle the question of salvation for many who never thought about it before.

But in shortening the journey towards spiritual wholeness, it also obscured our sense of the soul and of inner cleansing. Before this era began, an awareness of sin, self and God meant one thing. Afterwards, it meant something quite less. People were devoting and confessing and sanctifying they knew not what. The soul got lost in the assembly-line shuffle.

One might argue this idea of mass producing soul-less conversions played a huge role in the shaping of evangelism in that day, from Charles Finney's suggestion that "a revival . . . is a purely philosophic result of the right use of means," to Billy Sunday's boast that he could evangelize a community for the low cost of $4.92 a head.

Now here is where we get off. We cannot process sanctification wholesale and expect a radical change in anyone who buys it. And we cannot afford to ignore the Holy Spirit in the process, either. For sanctification to make any difference, we must first learn to wait on God.

Jesus often reminded His disciples that "no one knows the Father except . . . those to whom the Son chooses to reveal him" (Matthew 11:27); or that certain things are "not revealed to you by man, but by [the] Father in heaven" (16:17); or that "the Spirit gives life—the flesh counts for nothing" (John 6:63). That is, we cannot discover the truth about God or the gospel on our own, and we will never feel as though *we* are included until first, God moves on our hearts like He has had to move on every previous generation and convert. This is *His* game.

Another of the wonderful surprises in the Christian gospel is that God has not left us alone to carry out the task of living the perfect life, but "he who began a good work in you will carry it on to completion until the day of Christ Jesus" (Philippians 1:6). As Christians, we were given the Holy Spirit that first day we trusted in Christ, and it is only through *Him* that we desire and accomplish anything (see Philippians 2:13).

My observation has been that there are brief windows of opportunity in every believer's life when God's Spirit deals more intensely with us than at other times. And the wise Christian will learn to pay attention for these opportunities, and then to seize them. This is his defining moment, when he will ask to have his whole nature cleansed. Until such time, he will read his Bible or attend his church services with a new sensitivity, for God may have certain things prepared for him that He will only say once, and if he is always waiting for a time more convenient than the present to get serious about his faith, he could miss everything. God's Spirit *moves*. And sometimes He passes. So the frugal man does not fritter opportunities by waiting until he has run out of fun things to do before he is finally sanctified.

If Wesley was right, we cannot choose the day of our sanctification any more than we can choose the day of our natural death. But there *are* things we can do to hurry the day, or to make the dying easier. Let's look at a few of these.

First, we can discipline ourselves to read—no—*study the Bible* as though our lives depended on it. Because they do. We can eliminate other things in our schedule in order to squeeze this in. We can read it in between Sundays. We can follow along in our Bibles when they read it from the platform in church. We can use it for family devotions.

"Sanctify them by the truth," Jesus prayed, "Your word is truth" (John 17:17). This is still the formula. Even so, how many of us still err because we do not know the Scriptures?

Next, we can *pursue all the knowledge of Christ* that we can get our hands on. Since we learn what we love, and then love *more* of whatever we learn, we can stop bashing intellect and baptizing ignorance as though one always had to choose between the head and the heart. One wise writer from the past has promised that "Christ will never throw out what we have learned—if it is true—but set it on fire." Besides, most of us will find ourselves in the pages of another man's story, and this will inspire, or sometimes humble us to live the higher, simpler and deeper life.

Third, *we can honor the assembling of ourselves together*, and all the more as we see "the day" approaching. Since God speaks more often in oracles (public) than in visions (private), we can show up for church services with inquisitive minds. Since He has a history of hiding His truth in the conversation of others, we can ask more than we answer and listen more than we talk. Whatever message God has been trying to tell me is probably tucked inside the heart of another believer who is further along. And it may have already been said.

Fourth, *we can schedule "hour-long monasteries"* where we are alone with God. If we're busy (and who isn't these days?), we can look for the free time we already have. We can turn off the television. Shut down the computer. Turn off the radio and drive to work in silence. Put down the newspaper. Forget the good novel, if we must. Take walks. Take days off. Hunt. Fish. Sleep less. Whatever it takes. Because if you're going to live near the water, you'd better learn to swim, and if you're going to live near this fast-paced culture, you'd better learn to often withdraw to lonely places and pray (see Luke 5:16).

So we can steal an hour or two per week in the office, the woods, the attic, the car, or the lake, and read or conduct worship services that are *not* open to the public. We can sing. Pray. Reflect. Or ponder the attributes of God. Jesus did, and He needed to. So should we, for we can only see the bottom of our soul when the waters above it are calm.

Fifth, believing the definition of "deep" to be layer upon layer, and not just random profundity, *we can expose ourselves to great Christians of the past.* These men and women will speak of a life that is deeper than most things we have heard or sat beside in church recently. And the stimulus will do us good. Most writing today barely gets beneath the surface of spiritual matters because it is written to sell. It is clever, fast-paced, "verbal video," perfectly suited for a market whose reading level barely exceeds the fourth grade. The funny stories and cute illustrations are the literary form of dot-to-dot coloring books. And all of this appeases the modern mind which prefers never to read the text, but only to look at the pictures. We can consult the writings of earlier mystics like Augustine, Madam Guyon, Brother Lawrence, John of the Cross, Jeremy Taylor, and a host of others whose names we neither know nor can pronounce. They will tell us, in a sentence, what it took them a lifetime to learn, and we may find ourselves caught up in their yearning for holiness. And besides, the wisdom of God does not change every fifty years.

Sixth, *we can pray more and pray longer.* Most of us don't need to be taught to pray. We need to be shown it is necessary. And in matters of holiness, it is absolutely indispensable. A.W. Tozer was right, God is a person and, as such, must be encountered the same way as any other person—through time, conversation, and intimacy.[1] It is one thing to meet a man once. It is something else to read his biography. But it is a whole new experience to know the man about whom others only read or speak. Prayer is the one avenue that makes this happen, and through this it makes possible the crisis of sanctification.

Seventh, *we can travel in pairs,* because as Solomon observed, "if one falls down, his friend can help him up . . . [and] one may be overpowered, [but] two can defend themselves, and a cord of three strands is not quickly broken" (Ecclesiastes 4:10, 12).   We can join accountability groups that hold our feet to the fire.   We can risk vulnerability.   We can confess the true state of our souls, for better or worse, to a few trusted friends.   Then we can heed their advice in the particulars of our life.

Eighth, *we can take our religion literally* by doing the "little things." If the Scriptures say "look after orphans and widows" (James 1:27), we can create ways to take care of them. If they say "Love . . . with actions and in truth" (1 John 3:18), we can do it. Too often, we learn the art of explaining away the text on these minor things, and then apply these new skills to the greater texts on holiness and sanctification.

Ninth, *we can stay alert* for the moment when God is ready to sanctify us. We will get a sense of being at the crossroads, where we must decide our future. As a pastor, I have counseled those who say something is happening in their spiritual life, but they are not sure what it is. God has been waking them up in the middle of the night, or taking them away for hours during the busy afternoon to study the Scriptures. He has been flooding their emotions with everything from tears to laughter, and they want to know why.

"What does God expect from me?" they ask. "What does He want me to do?"

These are usually their defining moments. God is taking them to a point of decision, and they will never be here again. But it is possible that God is not asking them to *do* anything, but rather to *be* something more. These are often early tremors which lead to the crisis of entire sanctification. I have heard some testify that this defining moment was so clear, that they sensed to walk away from this blessing was to forfeit everything—even the religion they already had. Most impressions will not be this extreme, and even when they are, they must always come from the voice within us and never from those around us, preachers included.

On the other hand, I have counseled many who said the magic prayer, but wonder why nothing has changed.

"I went down to the altar and I let go of it," a woman says, confessing the bitterness that was holding her back, "but nothing happened. I still wake up in the middle of the night thinking about it. What's wrong?"

It wasn't time.

She cannot be entirely sanctified merely because one day she decides she should. She must wait and pay attention to the subtle voice of the Holy Spirit inside her, and then seize the opportunity when all of her yearnings have reached a critical point. If she jumps too soon, she will abort the process, then later believe that grace has failed her, and that *this* is as good as it gets.

It is no different for us. We, too, must wait for a defining moment in which we are pressed hard by God to choose between a radical holiness and the common religion of Everyman.

But what does this defining moment look like? Here are a few indicators:

> When you have reached a point where you can
> dig no deeper into your nature or the "why"
> of your sin; when you have seen the self that
> permeates everything you do and you have come
> to loathe it; when you are not just frustrated
> by your failures, but truly hate them; and
> when you can honestly say it is the *sin* you
> hate, and no longer only the guilt . . . *it is
> time for your sanctification.*

> When there is nothing you desire more than
> holiness; when you truly have but one holy
> passion and it is to be holy as Christ is
> holy; when you are obsessed with God and His
> likeness, and you would do *anything* to have
> a pure heart; when you are willing to forgo
> any pleasure, endure any hardship, sacrifice
> any convenience, risk any embarrassment,
> forgive any offender, obey any orders in order
> to please God; and when you will not let go
> until He blesses you . . . *it is time for
> your sanctification.*

> When your interest in the Word of God has
> passed from fascination into love; when you
> look forward to reading it; when you can
> truly say it is "more precious than gold"
> . . . *it is time for your sanctification.*

> When you have had a fresh awakening of God's
> love for you; when you feel chosen and
> singled out to be loved by Him; when you
> begin to grasp how wide, and how high, and
> how deep is the love of God, and you long

to show that love that surpasses knowledge;
and when you feel the pull of sin diminish
in the light of His love . . . *it is time*
for your sanctification.

When John Wesley insisted that sanctification (or "Christian Perfection" as he often called it) occurred sometimes months or even years after conversion, he could do so with the knowledge that we simply cannot bring these kinds of spiritual gains to our own life without the help of the Holy Spirit. And usually, this takes time.

"How are we to wait for this change?" asked Wesley. "Not in careless indifference, or indolent inactivity; but in vigorous, universal obedience; in a zealous keeping of all the commandments; in watchfulness and painfulness; in denying ourselves and taking up our cross daily; as well as in earnest prayer and fasting . . ." And when asked why so few ever received the blessing, he answered, "Inquire how many are seeking it in *this* way; and you have a sufficient answer."[2]

The difference between entire sanctification as I heard it in my early years, and as I see it in Scripture, is all in this matter of waiting on God, and in recognizing my opportunity rather than creating it. And this leads us into the second step we have labeled *seize the moment.*

Seize the Moment

Many potential gains will fizzle into good intentions if we only allow ourselves to *feel* these wonderful graces, but never to *act* on them. Every Sunday, thousands are stirred in church by the movement of God, yet they are unchanged when the fanfare is over. God has arrested them but, because it is not in His nature to do so, He has refused to take them hostage. And they themselves have never finally surrendered.

In some cases, this act of surrender is an acknowledgment of the fact that God has been cleansing us all along and has finished with the last stain, or that He has finally perfected our circle of Christian love, and from now on will only be enlarging it.

In other cases, this defining moment may take the form of a bold confession of faith whereby we, who have been growing all along, declare we are finally "filled to the measure of all the fullness of God (Ephesians 3:19), or that even though we have been dying to sin a little each day, we finally establish that the crucifixion is over (as it was for Paul, who spoke of it in the perfect tense), and from now on we will live for Christ . . . "by faith in the Son of God" (Galatians 2:20).

This is a critical moment. And we should not gloss over it just because we have seen it abused. For if we hold to a crisis of entire sanctification without the process of waiting on God, we are left (except in rare cases) with a sanctification of we know not what. We have merely confessed the cleansing of a heart not fully uncovered. But if, on the other hand, we pursue sanctification without finally seizing the moment and taking it for ourselves, then we are not really progressing at all, since all progress implies not only a destination, but an actual time of arrival somewhere down the road. Without either of these in this world, we are only wandering and not truly progressing. Or at best, we are merely biding time.

The defining moment, or "crisis" in our lives will involve a couple of things, and both will happen simultaneously. The first is *repentance*. We must remember, as a rule, that God will cleanse whatever we expose to Him, whether an act or a condition. So "woe is me," and not "what have I done?" is our concern here. We not only admit to having sinned, but to being a sinner and a rebel at heart. It is not that we told a lie or held a grudge or had an affair. It is that we have lived primarily for ourselves, that we have been "at home outside of God's presence, and absolutely unhappy in that presence," as Samuel Ridout put it. It is that we have built our own little kingdom and pulled the whole world in after us, until our careers, our spouses, our children, our pleasure, our values, and even our virtue all serve our personal interests, until our heart has become fossilized with pride. We do not typically see this at the time of our conversion, and so we cannot repent of it. But once we do, we are promised "a heart of flesh" and "truth in the inner parts" (Ezekiel 36:26; Psalm 51:6). Even those who have been Christian for years may one day awaken to learn that, while they have always obeyed the Scripture and submitted to the Lordship of Christ, their obedience was motivated by fear or duty, which makes them more slaves than heirs of God. These may repent that even though they obeyed, they did so reluctantly, and now that their eyes have been opened, they are free to serve God through the Spirit of sonship (Romans 8:15).

We may say a prayer. We may be anointed with oil. We may recite a creed. There may be signs and wonders. Or we may have none of these. The key is not the prayer or the oil or the signs and wonders. It is the will of the individual. Whenever our will is finally surrendered, together with all of the (albeit wholesome) things in life over which we have made it guardian, we are said to be sanctified—whatever else is or is not happening on the outside. We may recognize this moment or we may not. We may believe in the doctrine of entire sanctification or we may not. We may do cartwheels down the center aisle, or we may get up and leave quietly. It doesn't matter. Our sanctification depends on the complete surrender of our whole being, and not on these lesser things.

From this point, the only other thing required for our sanctification is faith. But this is no small item. And we may fake this in every place but heaven, where everyone knows better. For this reason, great Christians of the past often distinguished between real faith and its counterfeit, which is a hair still worth splitting. Real faith is not merely believing that God can cleanse us, but that He *will*. And there is a huge difference between the two. We must think of our faith, then, as the culmination of three stages.

The first is *knowledge*. For our faith to be genuine, we must first be informed, for no one can believe what he does not understand. We must learn and then believe that God has promised a pure heart and a perfect love to all of His people, and that He is capable of delivering what He promised. We must learn that the plan of God through the ages has been the holiness of His people. We must believe that our Christian walk is not a treadmill but a track, with a definite goal in view; that Christ, who authored our faith, will also perfect it. And we must believe that God desires to do this sometime before we die. Then we must learn exactly what is meant by it. That was our emphasis in chapter 6.

The next stage is *personal conviction*. We must not only believe that holiness is God's plan through the ages, but that it is His plan for us. This is where many fail.

"I believe God so loved the world," they say, "but I'm not so sure He loves *me*." They are after a personal invitation. They want an autographed copy of the Bible. And in this they desire more than any (but a scant few) before them have ever had. This is only pride and unbelief holding out for a better offer, and it had better expect none.

J. Sidlow Baxter once challenged God to prove his love by writing "God loves J. Sidlow Baxter" with clouds across the sky, but then quickly got to the heart of his problem when he confessed, "I would probably think there was *another* J. Sidlow Baxter somewhere else."

For this malady of unbelief, the Scripture only suggests that "faith comes from hearing . . . the word of Christ" (Romans 10:17). John Calvin said that faith and the Word of God "can no more be separated (from each other) than rays of light from the sun." As implausible as it may seem, a constant soaking of the mind in the Scripture is the only way to get a little of it under our skin. Sooner or later, by the help of God, we will come to *believe* some of what we've read, and because we've read it, we'll have something of substance to believe.

Whenever and however it happens, genuine faith calls for the belief that God intends for each of us what He has written in the pages of Scripture.

The third stage of faith is *reliance*. This is the culmination of all our belief up to this point. We may know what holiness is. We may believe that God is capable of sanctifying whomever He chooses. We may even believe He is capable of sanctifying *us* if He wants to. Or even more, that He will someday. But until we claim it for ourselves, we will, at best, possess it unknowingly, or worse, possess it not at all. We may be sanctified without believing in the doctrine, but never without believing in the act. Repentance and faith have always been the hinges upon which every blessing from God has turned, as every Protestant since the Reformation will tell you.

"Faith is the condition, and the only condition of sanctification," Wesley said, "no man is sanctified until he believes, [and] every man, when he believes, is sanctified."

And so these two, repentance and faith, are the two indispensable elements which lead to our sanctification. And always in this order. For if one believes he *has* the good life before he repents, he is only deceiving himself and ruining the image of holiness in front of others who are always watching.

Reform Our Lifestyle

After we have dealt with these two elements, repentance and faith, all that remains for us to do is to reform ourselves to match our profession of faith. John told us to "walk in the light as [Christ] is in the light," because the "blood of Jesus . . . purifies us from all sin" (1 John 1:7). Paul told us to "live a life worthy of the calling [we] have received" (Ephesians 4:1), and to "live up to what we have already attained" (Philippians 3:16). This is where the spiritual disciplines come in. Like food and water, they cannot create the new life, but they can certainly strengthen it. In fact, without them we will die. So immediately following our sanctification, and even before it, we should learn the disciplines of prayer, meditation, confession, solitude, worship, stewardship; or even the more radical ones like fasting, chastity or silence. These are a wake up call to the soul that is too easily satisfied with the ordinary.

But it is critical to follow the sequence here.

First: repentance.

Second: faith.

And third: reformation.

Confuse these, and we will end up with shallow conversions (which is faith before repentance), or legalism (which is reformation before faith). Many are the miserable who have fallen into one of these extremes. But if we are faithful to search our hearts, risk our faith and reform our lifestyles, we can live in the grace that God has promised.

There's an old saying, "If a cat sits on a hot stove, he will never sit on a hot stove again . . . but then, he will never sit on a cold one either."

This has been the story of my generation who has been so damaged by counterfeit holiness, so as never to desire it at all. Many have yielded themselves to God, only to find a nagging desire for more. They want it, but because of past experiences, have not allowed themselves to believe it is possible.

"Crisis? What crisis?" they say, and solemnly hold to a struggle theology with no relief this side of heaven. Yet, somewhere in the back of their minds is the persistent voice of Scripture, and the inspiring testimonies of men and women whose words they have no reason to doubt, that the very best of God is somewhere nearby, and that it doesn't need to be discovered, so much as truly believed. Then one day, with minds no less objective than any of their critics, they will look back and know that God has done immeasurably more than all they could ask or imagine . . . but always according to the faith within them.

NOTES:
[1] A.W. Tozer, *The Pursuit of God*, (Harrisburg: Christian Publications, 1961), p. 50.
[2] John Wesley, *A Plain Account of Christian Perfection*, (Louisville: Pentecostal Publishing), p. 25.

CHAPTER **11**

HABITS OF THE HOLY

How to Know You're Sanctified

It's May again.

Time for our annual reports.

Every year, we are asked by our denomination to report the "number of persons sanctified this year through local church ministries."

What does this mean?

For instance, shall we count how many prayed, or how many meant it? This is a fair question these days.

And how do we know who meant it? Shall we measure the intensity of the seeker at the altar? Or the radical change to his or her lifestyle a year later?

But how do we measure intensity?

And what if there are radical changes, but we never saw him repent? Does this count?

Or worse, what if he prayed and didn't change much at all? Shall we count *that*? Or shall we cross him off the list before we report him in May?

And what if we've already reported him? Do we start the next year with one in the hole? Or do we add a new category called: "total number of sanctified who petered out"?

Let's face it. When we count the number of those saved or sanctified for annual reports, we are really counting good intentions, and *only* good intentions. How can we know for sure? Plagued by these questions, we are moving fast into an era when no one is counting. This horrifies some, who have learned, over the years, to measure success by graphs and commendations. Church officials dread the day when pastors no longer count their converts, for fear they will then no longer *win* them.

Yet I have begun to wonder, as I look over the past 200 years of revivalism, if some of this counting business is related to a deeper issue. Could it be that we believe, in the back of our minds, that counting and assurance are somewhat related? Could we believe that to be counted by the shepherd is to be numbered among the sheep?

The early history of revivals has been that of sudden, dramatic, and definite conversions. Thousands who once had no interest in religion, were suddenly smitten with the idea of a holy God and reduced, then and there, to repentance. Skeptics, backsliders, hecklers, or curiosity seekers were saved in the twinkling of an eye, and the difference between the before and after was clear and unmistakable, or as one observer put it, there was no cheap grace in early revival.

Now who could mistake this? The children of revival were genuinely changed and they knew it. Everyone else knew it too. And right there is the problem.

It is possible that many of us, whose theology and experience is still rooted in revivalism, believe that as long as we can *know* if people are saved or sanctified, then we have the right to count them. And as long as we can count them . . . we can know. As one reads the stories of great revivals since the second awakening (1800-1820), he is struck with the number of references to how many were saved or sanctified in a given meeting. The ambivalent "many sought help" reports of Wesley's day slowly evolved into the "500 were sanctified" descriptions a generation later. According to one biographer, "Mrs. Maggie Van Cott . . . has held seventy-five thousand converts by the hand at the altar who promised to meet her in heaven."[1] Peculiarly, the frontier revivals were the one phenomenon separating Wesley's reporting from Mrs. Van Cott's.

So in a very subtle way, our numbers are not a simple way of reporting the progress. They are a form of quality control, in which the high priest reports the number of healed lepers, whose cleansing he endorses.

But as I said, we are moving out of this era, and into another that is less influenced by the miracle conversions of the past. There are now several shades of gray dividing the once clearly marked territories of sin and salvation. And very few seem to leap suddenly from one category to the other like they did a hundred years ago. And what is more, the power to declare that we are in one or the other no longer lies in the established church, but in the individual himself, who is supposed to know better.

In the past, the seekers sought sanctification until, one day, they "prayed through" with people in the church. From this point forward, they were treated as sanctified, and counted in the annual report. These were the predominant methods of knowing who was and wasn't sanctified over the last 100 years or so. First, we were counted, and then we conducted ourselves in accordance with very specific rules and observances, which usually came easier with age.

It was simple. . . clean . . . and definitive.

But not anymore.

So what do we do now? How do we know? Is there any evidence left to determine whether or not we are sanctified? What are the habits of the holy? Are there any that are *not* connected to the culture or the age?

Yes, there are. And the purpose of this chapter will be to examine them, in order that we may confirm "that Christ Jesus is in [us] . . . unless, of course, [we] fail the test" (2 Corinthians 13:5).

1. Is my conscience clear or exhausted?

Be careful!

Both conditions feel the same.

"Clear" means there is no rub of the good against the evil.

"Exhausted" means there is a callous where the rub has been going on for years.

Daniel Steele, a holiness theologian of the last century, taught us that a man's conscience has three capacities: (1) to discriminate between good and evil; (2) to supply him with an impulse to do what is right; and (3) to approve or disapprove his behavior. He also pointed out that a genuine conversion only slightly improves the first capacity, but greatly improves the second and third. This being true, the new believer is at a tremendous advantage in his struggle against sin if he will only learn to listen to his conscience. And once his heart is pure, his advantage is even greater. For a man's conscience is a sort of "central nervous system" to his soul, which stores his convictions, then feels the pain of anything which violates them, and keeps on throbbing until the pressure is relieved. Like any injury, we can deaden the pain for awhile and keep on playing, but sooner or later we will have to deal with it, or risk permanent damage. So even though I feel pretty secure in my relationship with God, it is a good idea, occasionally, to go back and ask myself the tough questions.

> Is there any sin or evil in my life that I have
> come to tolerate?

> Are my motives pure? Do I do *everything* to the
> glory of God alone?

> If my thoughts were a movie, could I let my seven-year-
> old daughter watch it?

> Have I treated others today the way Christ would
> treat them, given the same circumstances?

> Is my laughter and sorrow pure, or does it reflect
> another agenda?

The Living Bible says "a man's conscience is the Lord's searchlight, exposing his hidden motives" (Proverbs 20:27). It is wise then, for him to learn to listen to it. This is close to what Wesley labeled "the witness of the Spirit," which he said was "the testimony of our own conscience that God has given us to be holy of heart, and holy in outward conversation."[2]

Nevertheless, a guilty conscience is the mother of invention, as one comic pointed out. So many of us, myself included, have learned to sedate our consciences while we hold to the profession of a sanctified life.

Suzannah Wesley (John's mother) said, "Anything that weakens my reason, obscures my sense of God, or impairs the sensitivity of my conscience" [is] a sin.

We are not talking here of an ambiguous guilt that somehow God cannot be happy with us. This is usually a hangover from an earlier relationship with critical or non-accepting parents. Or worse, it is the accusation of the Devil, who is seeking to paralyze us. The conscience to listen to is the conscience that backs its accusations with solid evidence. If I feel guilty, but do not know why, I probably have less to worry about. But if my conscience tells me not only what I've done, but how it offended God, I'd better pay attention.

So is there any friction against the will of God within me? That is the question. There are some who are afraid to ask it, for fear it may turn up things which compromise their claim to holiness. But rest assured, the opposite is true. In my confession and repentance, I am helping my chances of holiness and not hurting them. For I am only squaring up with heaven, which has known the truth all along.

2. Is my religion an obsession or a hobby?

We must not confuse this holy passion with those who are naturally obsessive compulsive. The latter is largely a product of our culture. The former, of course, is not. So it would be as foolish to label every zealous person a saint today, as it was to label every epileptic a witch three hundred years ago. These natural zealots will only want to learn about the life of self-denial without ever entering it. And their interest is fleeting. They will soon lose themselves in the pro-life movement or in the National Rifle Association, like they appear now to have lost themselves in religion.

Nor is this an obsession over the many flags of the Christian church. As we have stated in the first chapter, holiness is not the passion to reform society—which is the heart of a crusader. It is not the hunger to know more about God—which is the heart of a theologian. It is not the vision to build a great church for God, nor even to win souls—which is the heart of an evangelist. And it is not a passion to express the eternal truths of God—which is the mantle of a preacher. A person may have all of these parts (good as they are), and never have captured the whole, which is the passion to take upon himself the very image of God—this is holiness.

So the questions we must ask ourselves are these:
Is my love for God occupying more and more of
my think-time?

Does it come up in my conversations more
frequently? Give examples.

Is there anything or anyone in the world more
important to me than Christ? Would I lose
it all before giving up my love for God? Do
other people know this?

Do I inspire others? Are people attracted to
holiness by the heat or "energy" of my
passion for God? Name them.

What have I sacrificed lately to further the
kingdom of God, or to tighten its grip on
my life? List the things.

The old-timers referred to this as "having a single mind." The writer of Hebrews called it "looking unto Jesus" (12:2 KJV). This is the one element that pushes us right to the edge. It makes us abnormal in a society where easy does it; where wisdom is measured in terms of moderation and anything more is considered extreme, or even insane. But if we truly desire to live the life of being holy men and women, and not just to talk about it, we will find ourselves marginalized by many whose company we used to enjoy. We will be out of step on earth, but perfectly in line in heaven (which is the world as we know it, upside down), because in our faith, grace has run its full course. God has been taken to His logical conclusion. The Cross has been returned to the realm of the miraculous.

3. Do other people say I am holy?

One side effect of those who worship independence (like Americans do) is the tendency to minimize, if not ignore altogether, the opinion others may have about us. But our holiness belongs to others as surely as a fire belongs to those people it warms. Whether enemies or friends, their opinion matters to God, so it should matter to me.

This is not the sole criteria, of course. They *can* be wrong. Our enemies can be too critical and our friends can be too soft. But if we could get them to be honest and fair for a moment, what would they say?

> Would my spouse say I am sanctified?
> > What evidence would be used to prove
> > that verdict?

> What would my children say? Have I ever asked?

> Is it possible my family speaks for God, and I
> > (in my self-criticism) am being too hard on
> > myself?

> Do the people at work know I am different? Is
> > it for better or worse?

> What evidence would my enemies use against me?

> Is there any substance, whatsoever, to the criticism
> > of the world? Is it enough to convict me?

It could be pointed out that, while Jesus' enemies hated Him, they did not misunderstand Him. Even after three years of bitter disputes with the religious leaders of His day, and only hours away from His crucifixion on charges of blasphemy, Jesus of Nazareth would have His righteousness vindicated on four separate accounts, regarding four of the most unlikely people: the Devil—"he has no hold on me" (John 14:30, Jesus referring to Satan); Pilate—"I find no basis for a charge against him" (John 18:38); the criminal next to him on the cross—"this man has done nothing wrong" (Luke 23:41); and the Roman centurion—"surely this was a righteous man" (Luke 23:47). And while His holiness was never acknowledged by some of His enemies, it was well known and feared by others who shrieked "Jesus of Nazareth . . . we know who you are—the Holy One of God" (Mark 1:24).

So were the Devil to accuse me before God (as he did Job), what evidence would he use? Would there be any substance to it? Let us never become so pompous in our piety that we disregard the word on the street. After all, if holiness is perfect love, then the world still has some right to determine whether or not we have it, since it was the criteria given them by God to know that we are His disciples (John 13:35).

4. Do I have power over sin?

Can I confidently say I will resist the next temptation, or do I only hope to? One is a resolve. The other, a mere preference.

> Do I hate sin as much as I loved the pleasure
> of it before?

> Am I attacking it? Or am I annexing it into
> my definition of holiness?

> Is there any sin that still has power over me?

It might be helpful here to distinguish between natural desires and sinful desires, because we often confuse them and are either too hard or too soft on ourselves.

Natural desires are those tendencies or inclinations which are part of our humanity. They are neither good nor evil, and they will stay with us from the cradle to the grave, no matter what progress we make toward sanctification. These are the basic needs of security, significance, love and acceptance, intimacy and the like. To deny these is not to be sanctified, but detached from the rest of humanity. And to pray they vanish is to pray in vain, for God will never take away by grace what He gave us by nature. Everyone has these desires, sinner or saint. So we need to purify the means by which we satisfy them.

For instance, we will be tempted to satisfy the natural desire for security, with evil desires of materialism or stinginess. We are tempted to fulfill the natural desire for significance, through pride and power. We may be tempted to gratify our wholesome need for love and acceptance through promiscuity. In any case, our real enemy here is not the natural desire, but the evil desires which flow from it. Pure ambition and selfish ambition both have their roots in our search for significance. Lifetime marriages and one-night stands both have their origins in our need for intimacy.

Even after our sanctification, we will be tempted to gratify completely normal desires with selfish means. But we will not cooperate, because we are controlled by the mind of Christ from the inside, and the desire to please Him is greater than the desire for anything else. We will still be tempted, but the temptation begins to flow from a different source. The temptations of sanctified people are not the temptations of a greedy heart bent on pleasing itself. They are not rooted in rebellion. They are the tempting of ordinary and innocent desires with extravagance, foolishness, or excess.

There is a certain point between the earth and moon where a rocket no longer needs its thrusters to push itself away from the earth. Having entered into the moon's own gravitational pull, it is drawn, gently at first, and then with more and more intensity until it has finally reached its destination.

There is also a point between sin and Christian perfection in which the believer no longer worries himself with falling, but, instead, is drawn by a fascination with the likeness of Christ. He is no longer propelled by the law; he is drawn by love. And whether or not he has truly reached it is another of many questions he may use to confirm his sanctification.

5. Do I have perfect love?

The old-timers used to say "like begets like." By that, they meant when we are truly sanctified, we bear the image of God, and God is love. And we not only love God, but others as well. And we sacrifice for them.

Just as the man of 1 Corinthians 13 may possess all of the gifts, but is "nothing" without love, so a person may possess all the attractions of the sanctified life, but is nothing unless he has love. In fact, without it he is a nice devil.

"Thought, purpose, logic, industriousness, but without radiance or love . . . think of it," says William Sullivan, "Isn't that an accurate description of Satan?"

So love is what makes God a person, and the rest of us a Christian at all. But what is love? Or more specifically, what is perfect love? It is loving God with *all* of our heart, soul, mind and strength; and having all of our thoughts, words and actions governed by love. Writes Wesley,

> There is nothing higher in religion—there is, in effect, nothing else. If you look for anything but more love, you are looking wide of the mark . . . . And when you are asking others, "Have you received this or that blessing?" if you mean anything but more love, you mean wrong. You are leading them out of the way, and putting them upon a false scent. Settle it then in your heart, that from the moment God has saved you from all sin, you are to aim at nothing more, but more of that love described in [Scripture]. You can go no higher until you are carried into Abraham's bosom.[3]

If we were to use only one question to settle the matter of sanctification in our minds, this is it. If we wonder what it is or who has it, we need look no further than this matter of perfect love. So . . .

> When was the last time I returned good for evil?

> Who are the enemies I pray for? Have I truly forgiven them, or do I simply avoid them?

> Am I unselfishly supportive of people who do better than me? Am I as encouraging to others when I lose as when I win? (Love for the weak and oppressed only appeals to our pride without challenging it.)

> When I am overlooked, or when I am robbed of the credit I deserve, can I let go of the glory? Think of a time.

> Am I considerate of others? Do I humbly adapt to whatever culture I am in?

> Am I sympathetic and benevolent? Who have I helped lately?

Augustine said, "Love has hands to help others . . . feet to hasten to the poor . . . eyes to see misery and . . . ears to hear the sighs and sorrows of men."

6. Do I have a genuine joy?

One powerful reminder of our sanctification is an undercurrent of joy, the absence of which is "practical atheism," for joy is as native to the attitude of a holy person as faith is to his mind. Together with love, joy is one of a few attributes to which mortals can relate. A higher principle or a gracious act may be kind or holy or gentle, but never joyful. Joy is the peculiar property of a *person*. And so it is one of the attributes that makes God a person, and people godly.

As one explores creation—whether the majestic mountains or the delicate blossoms of spring; whether the canyons of Arizona, the deserts of Egypt, or the rain forests of Brazil—he discovers the world has a rugged and random beauty all its own. It was not the work of Someone who was all business. It was, and is, the artistic expression of joy let loose. Whoever did it, had fun.

So joy is the personality of God. This partly explains why He is often portrayed, in the parables of Christ, as the Host of a huge celebration.

But more than this, joy is the color and animation to the Christian life, and only those deep into the life will ever know it. Those who play on the edges will only sense the misery of self-restraint. But those who throw themselves hard into their Christianity will learn how great a good religion is.

David expected the "joy of [God's] salvation" to return again, once his heart was pure (Psalm 51:10, 12).

Christ was preoccupied with it, as was Paul, who referred to it forty-five times in eight epistles, and called it the "fruit of the Spirit" (Galatians 5:22) and the "kingdom of God" (Romans 14:17).

Later, it was true of Christ's apostles, who faced the Sanhedrin, and then the lions in Rome. It was true of early Christians who burned, singing at the stake. It was true of early Methodists who were known for shouting in the middle of services. It is true of modern Christians who sit amidst poverty and harsh conditions and sing while they serve communion. It is one half of the "chief end of man."

E. Stanley Jones called it "swallowing sunshine," and C.S. Lewis, "the serious business of heaven," and G.K. Chesterton, "the gigantic secret of the Christian life." But what is it, really?

It is the laughter of the soul. It is an undercurrent of confidence that we are right with God and one with Him. It is a perfect contentment with our circumstances, because we believe they are ordered of God. It is unshakable trust.

Under the influence of joy, suffering still hurts, but it galvanizes our faith into loyalty. Discipline is still unpleasant, but serves to remind us we are sons, for "the Lord disciplines those he loves" (Hebrews 12:6). Persecution still seems unfair, but now it is no longer the random sadism of the gods, but a sacred rite of passage into the fellowship of Christ's sufferings (Philippians 3:10).

The Jewish philosopher, Martin Buber, told of a man who was afflicted with a terrible disease, and complained to his rabbi that his suffering was interfering with his studies.

"How do you know, friend, what is more pleasing to God? Your studying or your suffering?" said the rabbi.

So . . .

> When I am suffering, do I grumble or sing?
>
> Am I usually pleasant to be around?
>
> Am I confident about my relationship with God?
>
> Do I learn from my suffering? What have I
> learned lately? Do I accept it as a
> sacrament or scorn it as a curse?
>
> When was the last time I felt overcome with
> emotion towards God as I worshiped Him?
> How did I express it?

Joy is the consequence of a heart that has quit arguing, and finally settled down with God. And while it may not be the litmus test that perfect love is, it is a plausible way to measure the return on my investment into the Christian faith.

"Never let anything steal your joy," my father is fond of saying. And to the extent that it does, I may question or confirm my sanctification.

To Dr. Evan O'Neill Kane, of New York City, goes the dubious honor of being the first known surgeon to operate on himself. The sixty-year-old veteran removed his own appendix in 1921, not because he needed to, but because he wanted to prove that major operations could be performed under a local anesthesia. Finding no volunteers, he volunteered himself . . . because he believed in his theory.

Would to God that all who profess sanctification yield themselves as willingly to the scalpel of Scripture and Spirit. For the same Spirit who promised to bear witness with our spirit also warned us not to think more highly of ourselves than we ought (see Romans 12:3), that is, to conduct a form of surgery on ourselves, not because we are skeptical or enjoy a good clubbing every now and then, but because we believe in our faith enough to test it, and we love our God enough to ask Him for the truth.

"If anyone thinks he is something when he is nothing," warned Paul, "he deceives himself, [so] each one should test his own actions" (Galatians 6:3-4).   This fine line which separates confidence from deception can be drawn, without injury, down the soul of any person who is willing to examine himself regularly. If he does, he cannot be far wrong. And if he does not, he cannot be long right. It is as natural for holy people to examine themselves as it is for healthy people to schedule a physical. Not because they intend to fail the exam, but because they hope—if something *is* wrong—to catch it in the early stages.

These grueling examinations are never pleasant, but always worth it. So let us risk it. Let us take God more seriously than we take ourselves. Let us submit to His truth rather than barricade ourselves at a safe distance. Let us cherish the Word of God more than debate it . . . in order that we may be sons and daughters of our Father in heaven, and may one day know more fully the God we have come to love so far.

NOTES:
[1] A.M. Hills, *Holiness and Power*, (Cincinnati: Revivalist Office, 1897), p. 342.
[2] See Wesley's sermon, "The Witness of the Spirit" (Discourse I).
[3] John Wesley, *Plain Account of Christian Perfection*, p. 48.

More Holiness Resources from Wesleyan Publishing House

BKAM95　　　　　　　　　　**Leader's Guide**
　　　　　　　　　　　　　　　　BKAM68

Holiness for Ordinary People describes personal holiness in an understandable, life-related manner.

Dr. Keith Drury reflects on living in these changing times while holding true to the timeless message of holiness. This material is ideally suited for Sunday school or small group study. Learn how you can enjoy living a holy life today!

Who says you can't live like Jesus?

STEVE DeNEFF

M⊕RE
Than
Forgiveness

*A Contemporary Call to Holiness
Based on the Life of Jesus Christ*

BKB729

Steve DeNeff is convinced that ordinary people can live extraordinary lives—just as Jesus did.

Holiness is not conformity to a standard but abandonment to the love of God. Discover the beauty of a life completely surrendered to God! This is a book for anyone seeking the inspiration to live as Jesus did.

- God can make you *want* to do good
- Loving God is an all-consuming passion
- Your *direction* matters more than your *position*
- People who love what God loves must hate what He hates
- Living as Jesus lived will set you apart from the world